Dash Diet Cookbook for Beginners

1500 Days of Tasty and Healthy Low Sodium Recipes to Finally Reduce Your Blood Pressure - 30-Day Heart-Healthy Meal Plan Included

By

MATILDA GRIFFITH

Table of Contents

Introduction

When it comes to dieting, sometimes the hardest part is actually making the change. However, with a new understanding of healthy eating and keeping tabs on your calories, you can finally shed those extra pounds and see some major progress in your overall health. The number of people with high blood pressure, excess body fat, heart disease, and other ailments has been on the increase lately. This Dash Diet cookbook offer you the perfect way to solve this issue because it fills your plate with healthy fruits, vegetables, and lean meats.

The Dash Diet, also called Dietary Approaches to Stop Hypertension, is a low-sodium diet rich in fruits and vegetables. It is one of the only diet plans that has been clinically proven to reduce blood pressure. It is based on the fact that almost all disease-causing inflammation in the body starts with what we eat, because most diseases are associated with chronic inflammation. This diet focus on Anti-inflammatory lifestyle and the idea is to have healthy eating habits, which will ultimately result in a healthy living.

The DASH diet is an essential way to lower blood pressure, lose weight, and reduce the risk of many health problems like heart disease, cancer, diabetes and even dementia. They are not only tasty but also rich in vitamins and minerals that are essential for a healthy body.

Unlike other diets that focus on food restriction, this diet focuses on an eating pattern that promotes healthy living. This means that you eat a lot of fruits and veggies which help limit your intake of unhealthy that causes inflammation. The reason the Diet is used as a lifestyle is to replace all processed foods in your diet with more fiber-rich foods, like fruits and vegetables.

The Dash Diet has been proven by several studies to significantly decrease blood pressure, up to 10 points, as well as reduce weight and LDL ("bad") cholesterol. That is why it is recommended by the American Heart Association.

Eating a healthy and balanced diet is not an easy thing to do. But the Dash Diet can help you achieve your health goals and its recipes are easy to make as well. You can prepare delicious dishes for the whole family without spending too much time in the kitchen.

Adopting a healthy eating pattern is essential to get rid of excess weight, lower blood pressure and other health problems that are associated with unhealthy foods. The Dash Diet is an essential way to kick start your new healthy lifestyle. It will help users get rid of the active inflammation and prevent further diseases. You will have more energy and feel better while your body is getting healthier every day.

What is Dash Diet?

The Dash diet is a diet that has been scientifically proven to be more than twice as effective at reducing blood pressure levels when compared to a diet low in total fat. It utilizes the scientific principal of Load and Offset, which means that you will load your plate with whole grains, vegetables, and healthy proteins for six days out of a week and then fast for one day. This will help you maintain a healthy metabolic rate while also keeping your blood pressure under control. The principal of the diet comes from a long-term research study called the Dietary Approaches to Stop Hypertension (DASH) study.

The Dash diet was developed by the National Heart, Lung, and Blood Institute as a way to fight high blood pressure and heart disease. According to the American Heart Association, 90% of Americans are unknowingly hypertensive. High blood pressure is known as "the silent killer" because it usually has no obvious symptoms and often goes undiagnosed until damage is done to your cardiovascular system.

The aim of the Dash diet is to reduce the amount of salt (sodium) in food. In addition, it recommends eating foods that are high in potassium, calcium, magnesium and certain vitamins, such as A, C and E. Researchers believe that the sodium in our diets causes hypertension by raising the blood pressure. The more salt in our diet, the higher our blood pressure rises. And this may result into a variety of health issues over time, including heart disease and stroke.

The Dash diet is based on two principles: **1)** a low-salt (or "balanced") diet rich in fruits and vegetables, which includes a measure of lean protein foods (e.g., meat, poultry, fish and eggs) but no more than 30% of total daily calories from saturated fat; and **2)** physical activity to promote good cardiovascular health.

A healthy diet must contain 2,300 mg of sodium or less per day for good health. It is meant to be a low-sodium diet that provides more than the minimum recommended amount of potassium, calcium and magnesium.

By reducing sodium in the diet and increasing potassium, phosphorus and magnesium intake, the Dash diet can help lower blood pressure. If people follow this diet for two or more years, blood pressure can be reduced by an average of 5 mm Hg systolic and 2 mm Hg diastolic. In addition, a recent study found that lowering sodium intake is associated with a greater reduction in systolic blood pressure than lowering saturated fat or total fat.

Besides lowering blood pressure, the Dash diet may also help improve sleep and mental health. A review of clinical trials published in 2012 suggests that the Dash diet improves delta sleep scores and quality of life in people with hypertension compared to a diet that is lower in potassium and phosphorus.

The Dash diet was originally recommended for patients who were already on medications for high blood pressure, but it can be prescribed to healthy individuals as well. For lowering high blood pressure, it has become one of the most popular diets on the market.

The diet can be administered in a number of different ways. Most commonly, it is administered as part of a weight loss plan as the Dash diet is often associated with low-calorie diets. In addition, some people follow the Dash diet to lower their blood pressure (alone), and still others use it to lose weight, improve mental health and sleep quality (a combination of the above).

Benefits of Dash Diet

The Dash Diet is one of the easiest ways to improve your overall health and lose weight. It contains a lot of fresh vegetables and fruits, whole grains, lean meats, and low-fat dairy products. The diet has been proven to influence the body in numerous ways such as:

a) **Healthy Weight Loss:** Studies show that eating healthy is the key to weight loss. The Dash Diet has been shown to lower blood pressure in obese people as well as improve their cholesterol levels and help them lose weight. The Dash Diet will help you to lose weight more quickly than other diets because it has fewer calories but still contains all the nutrients your body needs to stay healthy.

b) **Improved Cholesterol Levels:** The Dash Diet works to lower your total blood cholesterol level by 1%. Also, it has been proven that the more closely you follow this diet, the more effective it is. So, by following this diet plan, you can reduce LDL and raise HDL numbers to a greater effect than eating a typical American diet. By lowering high blood pressure and cholesterol, you'll prevent heart disease from starting or worsening.

c) **Weight Loss:** The Dash Diet has been proven to help you lose weight. One study showed that when participants started eating healthy and exercised regularly, they lost weight and lowered their risk for heart disease. To some extent, eating healthy is key to weight loss. Such as reducing caloric intake and increasing physical activity.

d) **Improved Blood Pressure:** The Dash Diet has been proven to lower blood pressure in people with hypertension as well as those with pre-hypertension. Eating healthy works to reduce your blood pressure; it also prevents heart disease and stroke. The diet is recommended for people who have high blood pressure, pregnant women, diabetics and those who are at risk of developing high blood pressure.

e) **Improved Blood Sugar Levels:** The Dash Diet will also help improve your blood sugar levels by eating foods that are low in carbohydrates (the key nutrients for maintaining normal blood sugar). It has been shown to help people lower blood pressure, lose weight, and prevent heart disease and other chronic diseases. The diet has also been proven to help reduce the risk of developing diabetes by lowering AGE levels, which are associated with many chronic diseases.

f) **Better Cholesterol Levels:** With the Dash Diet, you'll enjoy higher HDL levels than those who follow a normal diet. It has also been shown to lower LDL cholesterol and triglycerides. It also helps raise HDL levels. Triglycerides can cause inflammation and plaque formation in arteries, which increases your risk for heart disease and stroke.

g) **Lower Risk of Chronic Diseases:** The DASH Diet is the best way to lower your chronic disease risk. Eating healthy foods will improve all aspects of your health in numerous ways. The Dash Diet has been proven to lower blood pressure and cholesterol levels for healthy people, prevent heart disease and diabetes. This diet is also proven to improve body composition, which can reduce the risk of cancer and other chronic diseases.

h) **Improved Sleep:** The Dash Diet improves sleep quality in a way that other diets fail to do. People who stick to the eating plan sleep better than those who don't, according to research. This may be because it improves mood and serotonin levels. The diet plan also helps reduce inflammation and oxidative stress, which can also cause trouble sleeping.

Dash Diet Food List with Low Sodium

1. **Vegetables:** you should aim for at least 45 percent of your meals to include a vegetable. such as: leafy greens, broccoli, kale or collard greens asparagus, celery and cucumbers, steamed spinach or green beans, Eggplant is also an excellent low-sodium option.

2. **Fruits:** apples, apricots, cherries, grapefruit, honeydew melon, oranges, tangerine, and Pineapple. Avocado is good because it is high in monounsaturated fat, protein and fiber. Bananas are also a good choice when eaten in moderation.

3. **Salad Greens:** romaine, iceberg, spinach, mixed greens, Mix of greens such as romaine mix green with spinach. Kale mixed with spinach. Greek salad is an excellent choice. Grilled vegetables are another good choice such as broccoli, carrots and bell peppers. Mushrooms are also a good choice because they are low in calories and are high in potassium and fiber content.

4. **Soy and Pea Products:** tofu, edamame, tempeh, miso, shoyu (soy sauce), tempeh are high or good sources of protein.

5. **Legumes:** soybeans, lentils, beans include phosphorous and fiber. They help lower the risk of type 2 diabetes by binding with cholesterols and raising the HDL (good) HDL cholesterol level. Grains are also good sources of protein and complex carbohydrates.

6. **Vegetable Broth**: is a good choice as long as it contains no added MSG especially those made from beans or vegetables should be consumed regularly.

7. **Nuts:** are also a good choice. Almonds are one of the best choices because they are low in calories and contain monounsaturated fat and protein. They are high in calories, protein, fiber and monounsaturated fat.

8. **Whole Grain:** Quinoa is a good choice to include on the diet since it is high in fiber, calcium and iron. Brown rice, and buckwheat are excellent sources of complex carbohydrates. Oatmeal, and other wholegrain bread can be consumed daily.

9. **Drinks (water):** Hydration is key to staying healthy because it motivates people to eat more fruits and vegetables, which are the only healthy options people can consume when they are not eating a low-carb diet. Drinking water is important. You should take a lot of water when on a low-carb diet since it acts as a satiety aid, preventing you from overeating. Water is a weight-neutral fluid but it helps curb appetite and prevents overeating. Drinking water before meals helps people eat less.

10. **Meat:** should still be part of your diet on the Dash diet, but in moderate amounts per day. The amount of meat you can eat depends on your sex and age. For women, it is recommended that consumption be 1 to 1.5 ounces of lean muscle-meat per day while men should consume two to three ounces a day.

11. **Fish and Poultry:** You can eat fish and poultry, but in limited amounts. One serving of fish is 3 to 4 ounces and one serving of poultry is the size of a deck of cards (about 3 ounces) or smaller than that. Studies have shown that consumption of seafood twice a week is beneficial for heart health, especially for younger women who are at risk for heart disease because they are more likely to have high LDL cholesterol levels. By adding seafood and poultry to your diet, you can lower your saturated fat intake.

12. **Dairy:** The only dairy sources you are allowed to consume on the Dash diet are fat-free or 1% milk or yogurt, low-fat cheese, cottage cheese, part-skim mozzarella cheese or soy products. Fat-free or low-fat dairy products are your best choice because they have less saturated fat than full-fat dairy.

13. **Vegetable oil:** One serving of vegetable oil contains roughly 30 calories and 8 grams of total fat. It contains polyunsaturated fat, which is a good type of fat and has been shown to reduce the risk of heart disease. The best products include: olive oil, canola oil, soybean oil and other types of cooking oils.

How To Get Started!

Eating healthy is hard. Finding the time and money for groceries can be difficult, and then there are all those recommended meals that are so expensive on a diet. But the Dash diet is one of the easiest ways to eat better on budget and it's also a great to lose some weight!

The Dash diet is a great way to get started with healthy eating. It teaches the daily recommended amount of carbs, fats, proteins and even sodium that should be available in each meal. They are Dash also a great weight loss plan, because it focuses on whole foods and low-glycemic load foods. These are foods that digest slowly when they hit your bloodstream. This means the food will release its nutrients slowly, so your blood sugar and hunger won't spike.

The main goal of the DASH diet is to get people away from processed foods, sugar, grains and sodium – since these are all the things that can be harmful to your body and lead to problems like type 2 diabetes, cancer and heart disease. The Dash diet also encourages eating healthy fats and not eating too many carbs – which are the two things our bodies burn the most related to energy.

The Dash diet is based on a vegan/vegetarian way of eating, but it doesn't actually require you to be vegetarian or vegan (which can be beneficial because it will cut down on processed foods and grains). You simply need to put yourself first and make sure you're getting plenty of healthy food. Though there are no specific time-frames or portion sizes – the main idea is that you're choosing lots of fruits and veggies, beans, nuts and whole grains. There should be a smaller amount of animal products and processed carbohydrates (like breads and pasta).

Now – let's talk about how to get started with this way of eating. The Dash diet won't be right for everyone, but if you've been looking for a healthier way to eat, this is a solid starting point. The Dash diet is also perfect for those who are looking for the whole foods approach to their diet so it's not too confusing. You can start by adding in Dash foods one at a time to your current diet – and see how it affects your weight and health when compared to not eating the Dash foods regularly.

Setting up your Dash diet is fairly easy. You'll take a few minutes to calculate your numbers. All you have to do is find out your daily recommended number of calories for weight loss and maintenance. For women 2,000 and for men 2,500 should be the daily calorie intake for weight loss (and 1,800 and 2,200 should be the daily intake for maintenance). Then you select your food list and set your Dash diet meals up. Next, set up your individual meal plans based on your carbs, protein and fat intake for each meal.

Once you've set up your individual meal plans, select the right recipes to see how they come together. You'll see a description of what to add in and picture of the recipes itself. Choose your meals and set them up in recipe book, write down the ingredients you'll need to purchase and get cooking! By letting you choose your favourite foods the diet makes it easier for you to find foods that fit your numbers, bill and then pile on the nutrients. These are choices you'll typically find in supermarkets, health food stores and even regular grocery stores.

Now that you've picked out some new Dash foods to try –it's important to remember you don't have to eat every single meal all day. Here's how to go about incorporating them into your diet. You can try to eat a Dash meal twice a day – or you can just make sure you're eating them every day. The key is to incorporate them into your diet as much as possible.

In order to do this successfully, it's important not to get too strict with yourself. While the Dash diet does recommend staying away from processed foods and sugar, you don't necessarily have to give up all processed foods or sugar when you first start out. Because you're just starting out and have chosen to eat Dash diet foods – there's no reason to feel overwhelmed. You'll just be adding them into your diet – so stay calm and don't feel like you need to do too much at once.

To start eating the Dash foods consistently and keep track of your weight – you'll be amazed at how much healthier your body will become. Now that you know all of this, you're ready to start eating your new Dash diet foods. Here are some things you'll want to keep in mind when trying the Dash diet for the first time:

1. It's best to start out slowly. The Dash diet recommends starting out with one or two foods that you just try out here and there (you can start by eating them twice a week). If they make you feel great, go ahead and eat them every day.
2. The best time to start eating Dash diet foods is at breakfast and lunch. You can have a Dash meal for breakfast or lunch – and then for dinner you can eat what you'd like.
3. When you're first starting out on the Dash diet, just try to eat a few of the different types of foods. Don't try to get too strict with yourself if you don't like the taste of some of them (remember – they were healthy even before they became popular). You can always experiment with other foods later.

Now that you have all of the information it's time to make the Dash diet part of your life, it's time to give this diet a try. At start, it's really important to stay accountable to yourself. When you make a commitment to eat healthy in a new way, it takes a lot of discipline – so if you're not used to this type of food, it may take some time. Just remember – you choose the Dash foods for a reason (because they're good for you) – so if you don't like them, that's okay.

But what about if you do like the Dash foods? Great! Don't pay attention to what other people are saying or doing. Don't let others influence your decisions too much (especially when it comes to trying out the new diet). It's up to you to know what you like, so stay strong in your beliefs and make smart choices.

In addition to making smart food choices – it's important to be patient with yourself (and not get discouraged). It isn't easy to change the way that you eat – but if you're determined, then you'll be fine. Always remember that it doesn't matter how other people are eating – the only thing that matters is how YOU are eating. If you're eating healthy, then you know all you need to know about how to eat.

Breakfast Recipes

1. Eggs on Toast

Preparation Time: 10 mins
Cooking Time: 3 mins
Servings: 2

Ingredients:

- 2 large eggs
- 2 tsp. low-fat Parmesan cheese, grated
- 2 whole-wheat bread slices
- Freshly ground black pepper, to taste

Directions:
1. Create a hole at the centre of bread slice each with a biscuit cutter.
2. Heat a greased non-stick skillet over medium-low heat.
3. Arrange a bread slice in the skillet and carefully crack the egg in the centre of the hole.
4. Cook for about 30-45 seconds. Sprinkle with black pepper and carefully flip the slice. Cook for about 1 minute or until desired doneness of egg yolk.
5. Repeat with remaining slice and egg. Sprinkle with parmesan and serve.

Nutritional Fact:
Calories: 138, Carbohydrates: 10.8g, Sodium: 155mg, Fibers: 1.7g, Fat: 6.1g, Proteins: 9.9g

2. Healthy Buckwheat Pancakes

Preparation Time: 10 mins
Cooking Time: 30 mins

Serving Size: 2

Ingredients:

- ½ cup All-purpose flour
- ½ cup Buckwheat flour
- ½ cup Milk (fat-free)
- ½ cup Sparkling water
- 1 tablespoon baking powder
- 1 tablespoon Canola oil
- 1 tablespoon Sugar
- 2 Egg whites
- 3 cups Fresh sliced strawberries

Directions:

1. Add in the egg whites, milk, and canola oil into a small glass mixing container and whisk until all ingredients are well combined.
2. In another mixing container, add in the all-purpose flour, buckwheat flour, sugar, and baking powder and whisk together.
3. Add in the egg whites and water. Then whisk into a smooth batter-like consistency and set aside.
4. Take a non-stick griddle and place it over an average flame.
5. Grease it with non-stick cooking spray and let it heat through.

Nutritional Fact:
Carbohydrates: 24 g, Sodium: 150 mg, Fat: 3 g, Protein: 5 g

3.   Green Smoothie

Preparation Time: 2 mins
Cooking Time: 5 mins
Servings 4

Ingredients

- ½ cup Blueberries or blackberries
- ½ cup Strawberries
- 1 Banana
- 1 cup   Cold water
- 2 ounces fresh Baby spinach
- 4 tablespoons Lemon juice
- Fresh mint to taste

Directions:

1. Add in the banana, lemon juice, strawberries, blueberries or blackberries, baby spinach, fresh mint, and cold water into a blender and.
2. Blend into a smooth puree-like consistency.
3. Transfer into a tall glass and serve cold!

Nutritional Fact:
Protein: 1 g, Carbohydrates: 12 g, Sodium: 5 mg, Fat: 0 g

4.   Scallions Omelette

Preparation Time: 10 mins
Cooking Time: 10 mins
Servings 2

Ingredients

- ¼ teaspoon ground black pepper
- 1 oz scallions, chopped
- 1 tablespoon low-fat sour cream
- 1 teaspoon olive oil
- 2 eggs, beaten

Directions:

1. Heat up olive oil in the skillet.
2. Meanwhile, mix all remaining ingredients into a bowl.
3. Transfer the egg mixture in the hot skillet, flatten well and cook for 7 minutes over the medium-low heat.
4. Once set, the omelette is cooked.

Nutritional Fact:
Calories: 101, Proteins: 6g, Carbohydrates: 1.8g, fat: 8g, Fibers: 0.4g, Cholesterol: 166mg, Sodium: 67mg.

5.   Artichoke Eggs

Preparation Time: 5 mins
Cook Time: 20 mins
Servings 4

Ingredients

- 1 cup artichoke hearts, canned, chopped
- 1 tablespoon canola oil
- 1 tablespoon cilantro, chopped
- 1 yellow onion, chopped
- 2 oz low-fat feta, chopped
- 5 eggs, beaten

Directions:

1. Grease 4 ramekins with the oil.
2. Divide the remaining ingredients amongst the ramekins and bake at 350 degrees Fahrenheit for 30 minutes.
3. For 20 minutes, bake the meal at 380F.

Nutritional Fact:
Calories: 177, Proteins: 10.6, Carbohydrates: 7.4g, fat: 12.2g, Fibers: 2.5g, Sodium: 259mg.

6.   Overnight Refrigerated Oatmeal

Preparation Time: 5 mins
Cooking Time: 5 mins
Servings: 1

Ingredients:

- 1/3 cup Soy milk
- 1 ½ teaspoons dried Chia seeds
- ¼ teaspoon Cinnamon
- ¼ cup Rolled oats
- ¼ cup Greek plain yogurt (low-fat)
- ¼ cup Applesauce (unsweetened)
- ¼ cup Apples (diced)

Directions:

1. Add in the soy milk, unsweetened applesauce, rolled oats, low-fat Greek yogurt, diced apples, dried chia seeds, and cinnamon into a 500 ml glass cup with lid.
2. Close the lid and shake until they are nicely combined.
3. Place the glass cup into the refrigerator overnight.
4. Serve with fresh fruit toppings of your choice.

Nutritional Fact:
Carbohydrates; 30 g, Sodium; 89 mg, Fat; 4 g, Protein; 11 g

7.   Banana Bread

Preparation Time: 10 mins
Cooking Time: 1 Hour
Serves: 12

Ingredients

- 2 tsp. organic vanilla extract
- 2 eggs
- 1½ C. whole-wheat flour
- 1/3 C. fat-free milk
- 1 tsp. powdered stevia
- 1 Pinch of salt
- 1 C. ripe banana, peeled and mashed
- ½ C. unsalted walnuts, chopped
- ¼ tsp. ground cardamom
- ¼ C. canola oil

Directions:

1. Preheat the oven to 350 °F. Grease a 9x5-inch loaf pan.
2. In a large container, mix in flour, baking soda, stevia, cardamom, and salt.
3. In another container, add eggs, banana, milk, oil and vanilla extract and whisk until well combined.
4. Then, just until mixed, add the banana mixture to the flour mixture. Then include the walnuts into the mixture.
5. Transfer the mixture into prepared loaf pan and bake for about an hour.
6. Remove from the oven and put them on a wire rack to cool for 10 minutes. Also, Overturn the bread to cool on the wire rack before cutting.

7. Cut the bread into preferred sized slices and serve.

Nutritional Fact:
Calories: 155, Sodium: 14mg, Carbohydrates: 15.8g, Protein: 4.1g, Fibers: 1.1g, Sugar: 2.1g, Fat: 8.5g

8. Red Velvet Pancakes with Cream Cheese Topping

Preparation Time: 15 mins
Cooking Time: 10 mins
Servings: 2

Ingredients:
Cream Cheese Topping:
- 3 tbsps. Yogurt
- 3 tbsps. Honey
- 2 oz. Cream cheese
- 1 tbsp.

Milk Pancakes:
- 2¼tsps. baking powder
- 1 tsp. Vanilla
- 1 tsp. red paste food colouring
- 1 large Egg
- 1 c. + 2 tbsps. Milk
- ½ tsp. Unsweetened Cocoa powder
- ½ c. Whole wheat Flour
- ½ c. all-purpose flour
- ¼ tsp. Salt
- ¼ c. Sugar

Directions:
1. Combine all your topping ingredients in a medium bowl, and set aside. Add all your pancake ingredients in a large bowl and fold until combined.
2. Set a greased skillet over medium heat to get hot.
3. Add ¼ cup of pancake batter onto the hot skillet and cook until bubbles begin to form on the top.
4. Flip and cook until set. Repeat until your batter is done well. Add your toppings and serve.

Nutritional Fact:
Calories: 231, Proteins: 7g, Carbohydrates: 43g, Fats: 4g, Sodium: 0mg

9. Apple Oats

Preparation time: 5 mins
Cooking time: 5 mins
Servings: 2

Ingredients:
- 1 chopped apple
- 1 cup of water

- 1 tsp. of olive oil
- 1/2 cup of oats

- 1/2 tsp. of vanilla extract

Directions:
1. Add the oats to the saucepan with olive oil. Cook for 2 minutes while continuously stirring.
2. After that, mix in the water.
3. Cook the oats for 5 minutes on low flame with the lid closed.
4. Add the diced apples and vanilla extract after that. Toss the ingredients together.

Nutritional Fact:
Calories 159; Fat 5g; Carbohydrates 4g; Proteins 29g; Cholesterol 0mg; Sodium 6mg; Potassium 196mg

10. Easy Veggie Muffins

Preparation Time: 10 mins
Cooking Time: 40 mins
Servings: 4

Ingredients:
- Cooking spray
- A pinch of black pepper
- 4 eggs
- 3/4 cup cheddar cheese, shredded
- 2 cups non-fat milk
- 1 cup biscuit mix

- 1 teaspoon Italian seasoning
- 1 cup tomatoes, chopped
- 1 cup green onion, chopped
- 1 cup broccoli, chopped

Directions:
1. Grease a clean muffin tray with cooking spray and divide broccoli, tomatoes, cheese, and onions in each muffin cup.
2. In a bowl, combine green onions with milk, biscuit mix, eggs, pepper, and Italian seasoning, whisk well and pour into the muffin tray as well.
3. Cook the muffins in the oven at 375 degrees F for 40 minutes, divide them between plates and serve.

Nutritional Fact:
Calories: 80, Fat: 5g, Carbohydrates: 3g, Protein: 7g, Sodium: 25mg, Potassium: 189mg.

Lunch Recipes

11. Pistachio Mint Pesto Pasta

Preparation Time: 10 mins
Cooking Time: 10 mins
Servings 4

Ingredients
- Juice of ½ lime
- 8 ounces whole-wheat pasta
- 1 garlic clove, peeled
- 1 cup fresh mint
- ½ teaspoon kosher salt
- ½ cup fresh basil
- ⅓ cup unsalted pistachios, shelled
- ⅓ cup extra-virgin olive oil

Directions:
1. Prepare the pasta based on the package instructions. Drain, reserving ½ cup of the pasta water, and set aside.
2. In a food processor, add the mint, basil, pistachios, garlic, salt, and lime juice. Process until the pistachios are coarsely ground. Add the olive oil in a slow, steady stream and process until combined.
3. In a large container, mix the pasta with the pistachio pesto; toss well to combine.
4. If using a thinner, more saucy consistency is desired, add some of the reserved pasta water and toss well.

Nutritional Fact:
Calories: 420; Fats: 3g; Sodium: 150mg; Carbohydrates: 48g; Fibers: 2g; Proteins: 11g

12.   Shrimp with Asparagus

Preparation Time: 15 mins
Cooking Time: 10 mins
Servings: 4
Ingredients

- 4 garlic cloves, minced
- 2 tbsp. olive oil
- 2 tbsp. fresh lemon juice
- 1/3 C. low-sodium chicken broth
- 1 lb. shrimp, peeled and deveined
- 1 lb. asparagus, trimmed

Directions:
1. In a large clean frying pan with oil over medium-high heat, apply heat. Add all the ingredients except for broth and cook for about 2 minutes, without stirring.
2. Stir the mixture and cook for about 3-4 minutes, stirring occasionally.
3. Stir in the broth and cook for about 2-4 more minutes. Serve hot.

Nutritional Fact:
Calories: 225, Fats: 9.1g, Sodium: 280mg, Fibers: 2.5g, Sugars: 2.2g, Protein: 28.7g, Carbohydrates: 7.4g

13.   Stir-Fry Rice with Chicken

Preparation Time: 10 mins
Cooking Time: 30 mins
Servings: 4

Ingredients:

- A pinch of black pepper
- 2 tablespoons olive oil
- 2 garlic cloves, minced
- 1/3 cup rice wine vinegar
- 1 lb chicken breast dice into 1 inch cube
- ½ teaspoon ginger, grated
- ½ cup coconut aminos
- ½ cup chopped red bell pepper,
- ½ cup carrots, grated 1 cup white rice

Directions:
1. Heat-up a pan with the oil over medium-high heat, add the chicken, and stir for 4 mins on each side.
2. Add aminos, bell pepper, vinegar, black pepper, ginger, garlic, carrots, rice and stock. Cover the pan and cook over medium-heat for 20 mins.
3. Serve as a lunchtime meal by dividing everything into individual bowls. Enjoy!

Nutritional Fact:
Calories: 70, Carbohydrates: 13g, Fat: 2g, Protein: 2g, Sodium 5 mg

14.   Leeks Soup

Preparation Time: 10 mins
Cooking Time: 1 Hour And 15 mins
Servings: 6

Ingredients:

- Handful parsley, chopped
- garlic cloves, minced
- Black pepper to the taste
- 5 leeks, chopped
- 4 cups low-sodium chicken stock
- 3 tablespoons olive oil
- 2 gold potatoes, chopped
- 1 yellow onion, chopped
- 1 cup cauliflower florets

Directions:

1. Heat-up a pot with the oil over medium-high heat, add garlic and then onion, stir and cook for 5 minutes.
2. Add cauliflower, potatoes, leeks, black pepper, and stock, stir, bring to a simmer, then for 30 minutes cook over medium heat
3. Blend everything using an immersion blender, add parsley, stir, ladle into bowls and serve.

Nutritional Fact:
Calories: 125 carbohydrates: 29g Fat: 1g Protein: 4g Sodium 52 mg

15.   Indian Chicken Stew

Preparation time: 55 mins
Cooking time: 20 mins
Servings: 4

Ingredients:

- A pinch of black pepper
- 5 garlic cloves, minced
- 1-pound chicken breasts, skinless, boneless, and cubed
- 15 ounces tomato sauce,
- 1 tablespoon lemon juice
- 1 tablespoon garam masala
- 1 cup fat-free yogurt
- ½ teaspoon sweet paprika
- ¼ teaspoon ginger, ground

Directions:

1. Stir together the chicken and all of the other ingredients (except the yogurt and lemon juice) in a bowl and chill for an hour.
2. Toss the chicken mixture into a hot skillet and cook for 5-6 minutes, stirring occasionally.
3. Toss in the tomato sauce, garlic, and paprika, and simmer for 15 minutes more before dividing the mixture among plates and serving.

Nutritional Fact:
Calories 221, Fats: 6g, Fibers 9g, Carbohydrates: 14g, Sodium: 4 mg, Proteins: 16g

16.   Spinach Pork Cubes

Preparation Time: 10 mins
Cooking Time: 12 mins
Servings: 4

Ingredients
- 4 teaspoons spinach, blended
- 4 pork loin chops, cubed

Directions:
1. Mix up pork chops and blended spinach.
2. Then preheat the grill to 400F.
3. The meat cubes should be placed on the grill and grilled for six minutes on each side, or until the meat is browned and somewhat crispy on the outside.
4. Serve.

Nutritional Fact:
Calories: 256, Sodium: 57mg, Proteins: 18g, Carbohydrates: 0g, Fats 19.9g, Fibers: 0g

17.   Tilapia Casserole

Preparation Time: 10 mins
Cooking Time: 14 mins
Servings: 4

Ingredients
- 2/3 C. feta cheese, crumbled
- 1/3 C. fresh parsley, chopped and divided
- 4 (6-oz.) tilapia fillets
- 2 tbsp. fresh lemon juice
- ½ tsp. red pepper flakes, crushed
- ¼ tsp. dried oregano
- 2 (14-oz.) cans salt-free diced tomatoes with basil and garlic with juice

Directions:
1. Preheat the oven to 400 °F.
2. Using a shallow baking dish, add in the tomatoes, ¼ C. of the parsley, oregano and red pepper flakes and mix until well combined.
3. Arrange the tilapia fillets over the tomato mixture in a single layer and drizzle with the lemon juice.

4. Place some tomato mixture over the tilapia fillets and sprinkle with the feta cheese evenly. Bake for about 12-14 minutes.
5. Serve hot with the garnishing of remaining parsley.

Nutritional Fact:
Calories: 246, Sodium: 350mg, Carbohydrates: 9.4g, Fibers: 2.7g, Fat: 7.4g, Proteins: 37.2g, Sugar: 6g

18.   Easy Salmon Steaks

Preparation time: 10 mins
Cooking time: 20 mins
Servings: 4

Ingredients:

- Black pepper to the taste
- 4 cups of water
- 3 garlic cloves, minced
- 2 tablespoons olive oil
- 1 yellow onion, chopped
- 1 tablespoon thyme, chopped
- 1 lemon Juice
- 1 big salmon fillet, cut into 4 steaks
- ¼ cup parsley, chopped

Directions:
1. Place a pan with the oil on medium-high heat, cook onion and garlic within 3 minutes.
2. Add black pepper, parsley, thyme, water, and lemon juice, stir, bring to a gentle boil.
3. Add salmon steaks, cook them for 15 minutes, drain, divide between plates and serve with a side salad for lunch.

Nutritional Fact:
Calories: 110, Carbohydrates: 3g, Fat: 4g, Protein: 15g, Sodium 330 mg

19.   Lamb Curry with Tomatoes and Spinach

Preparation Time: 10 mins
Cooking Time: 12 mins
Servings: 4

Ingredients

- 2 Tbsp. Salt-free tomato paste
- 1 tsp. Olive oil
- 1, chopped Onion
- 3 cloves, minced Garlic

- Ground black pepper to taste
- 1, chopped red bell pepper
- 1 Tbsp. Salt-free curry powder
- ¼ cup Chopped fresh cilantro
- 1 pound sliced thinly Lean boneless lamb
- 10 ounces Fresh baby spinach
- ½ cup Low-sodium beef or vegetable broth
- ¼ cup red wine
- 1(15-ounce) can No-salt-added diced tomatoes

Directions:
1. Heat the oil in a pan.
2. Add lamb and brown both sides, about 2 minutes.
3. Add garlic, onion, and bell pepper. Stir-fry for 2 minutes. Add in and Stir the curry powder and tomato paste.
4. Add the tomatoes with juice, spinach, broth, and wine and stir to mix.
5. Stir-fry for 3 to 4 minutes and lamb has cooked through.
6. Remove from heat. Season with pepper and stir in cilantro. Serve.

Nutritional Fact:
Calories: 238, Sodium 167mg, Fat: 7g, carbohydrates: 14g, Protein: 27g

20. Honey Mustard Salmon

Preparation time: 5 mins
Cook time: 15 mins
Servings: 4

Ingredients
- 1 tbsp Honey mustard dressing
- 1lb (450g) 4 Salmon fillets

Direction:
1. Preheat the oven to 400F.
2. Arrange the salmon on a sheet pan coated with parchment paper. Cook in the oven for 10 minutes.
3. Remove from the oven and spread the honey mustard dressing over the salmon.
4. Return the sheet to the oven and bake for 5 minutes more. Serve.

Nutritional Facts
Calories: 167 Fat: 7g Carb: 1g Protein: 23g Sodium: 73mg

Dinner Recipes

---

21.   Lime Shrimp and Kale

Preparation Time: 10 mins
Cooking Time: 20 mins
Servings: 4

Ingredients:

- Zest of 1 lime, grated
- Juice of 1 lime
- A pinch of salt and black pepper
- 4 scallions, chopped

- 2 tablespoons parsley, chopped
- 1-pound shrimp, peeled and deveined
- 1 teaspoon sweet paprika
- 1 tablespoon olive oil

Directions:

1. Bring a clean pan to medium heat, add the scallions and sauté for 5 mins.
2. Toss in the remaining ingredients and simmer for an additional 15 minutes over medium heat before dividing into serving dishes and serving.

Nutritional Fact:
Calories: 149, Carbohydrates: 12g, Sodium: 250 mg, Fat: 4g, Protein: 21g

22. Quinoa & Bean Fritters

Preparation time: 10 mins
Cooking time: 25 mins
Servings: 3

Ingredients:

- ¼ tsp Ground cumin
- ½ tsp Kosher salt, divided
- ½ Small onion, chopped
- 1 can 15oz (420g) Chickpeas rinsed, and drained
- 1 cup cooked quinoa
- 1 Large egg
- 1 tbsp Olive oil, divided

Directions:

1. Heat 1 tspn of olive oil in a large skillet on the stovetop. Add the onion and 1/4 teaspoon of salt.
2. Sauté until translucent, about 4 minutes. Remove from the heat and allow the onion to cool.
3. In a food processor, combine the onion, quinoa, chickpeas, egg, cumin, and the remaining 1 teaspoon of salt.
4. Pulse until the mixture is combined.
5. In a clean skillet on the stovetop, heat the remaining 2 teaspoons of olive oil over medium heat. Working in batches, place 3 spoonsful of batter in the skillet and cook for 5 to 6 minutes per side.
6. Repeat to make 3 more fritters. Cook and serve.

Nutritional Fact:
Calories: 248 Fat: 9g Carb: 32g Protein: 10g Sodium: 377mg

23. Vegan Chili

Preparation Time: 15 mins
Cooking Time: 25 mins
Servings: 4

Ingredients:

- (1) 15-oz can red kidney beans, cooked
- ½ cup bulgur
- ½ cup celery stalk, chopped
- 1 chili pepper, chopped
- 1 cup low-sodium vegetable broth
- 1 cup tomatoes, chopped
- 1 teaspoon tomato paste

Direction:

1. Put all ingredients in the big saucepan and stir well.
2. Close the lid and simmer the chili for 25 minutes over medium-low heat.

Nutritional Fact:

Calories 234 Protein 13.1g Carbohydrates 44.9g Fat 0.9g Sodium 92mg

24. Shrimp with White Beans and Feta

Preparation Time: 15 mins
Cooking Time: 15 mins
Servings 4

Ingredients

- ¼ cup crumbled feta cheese, for garnish
- ¼ cup fresh mint, chopped
- ¼ cup no-salt-added vegetable stock
- ¼ teaspoon freshly ground black pepper
- ½ teaspoon kosher salt, divided
- 1 (15-ounce) can no-salt-added or low-sodium cannellini beans, rinsed and drained
- 3 tablespoons lemon juice, divided
- 1 large shallot, diced
- 1 pound shrimp, peeled and deveined
- 1 tablespoon white wine vinegar
- 1 teaspoon lemon zest
- 2 tablespoons extra-virgin olive oil, divided

Directions

1. In a small container, whisk together 1 tablespoon of the lemon juice, 1 tablespoon of the olive oil, and ¼ teaspoon of the salt. Add the shrimp and set aside.
2. In a large skillet heat what left of the olive oil or sauté pan over medium heat.
3. Add the shallot and sauté until translucent, about 2 to 3 minutes. Add the vegetable stock and deglaze the pan, scraping up any brown bits, and bring to a boil.
4. Add the beans and shrimp. Lower the heat, and simmer until shrimp are cooked through, about 3 to 4 minutes.
5. Turn off the heat and add the mint, lemon zest, vinegar, and black pepper. Stir gently to combine. Garnish with the feta.

Nutritional Fact:
Calories: 340; Fats: 11g; Sodium: 45mg; Carbohydrates: 28g; Fibers: 6g; Sugars: 3g; Proteins: 32g

25. Vegetarian Lasagna

Preparation Time: 15 mins
Cooking Time: 30 mins
Servings: 6

Ingredients:

- ½ cup bell pepper, diced
- 1 cup carrot, diced

- 1 cup low-sodium vegetable broth
- 1 cup spinach, chopped
- 1 cup tomatoes, chopped
- 1 eggplant, sliced

- 1 tablespoon olive oil
- 1 teaspoon chili powder
- 4 oz low-fat cottage cheese

Directions:
1. Put carrot, bell pepper, and spinach in the saucepan. Add olive oil and chili powder and stir the vegetables well. Cook them for 5 minutes.
2. Make the sliced eggplant layer in the casserole mould and top it with vegetable mixture.
3. Add tomatoes, vegetable stock, and cottage cheese. Bake the lasagna for 30 minutes at 375F.

Nutritional Fact:
Calories 77, Protein 4.1g, Sodium 124mg, Fat 3g, Carbohydrates 9.7g

26. Mussels and Chickpea Soup

Preparation Time: 10 mins
Cooking Time:10 mins
Servings: 6

Ingredients:
- 1 and ½ tablespoons fresh mussels, scrubbed
- 1 cup chickpeas, rinsed
- 1 cup white wine
- 1 small fennel bulb, sliced
- 2 tablespoons olive oil

- 3 garlic cloves, minced
- 3 tablespoons parsley, chopped
- A pinch of chili flakes
- Black pepper to the taste
- Juice of 1 lemon

Directions:
1. Using a medium-high heat, sauté the garlic and chili flakes in a large skillet with olive oil for a few minutes.
2. Cook for 3-4 minutes, stirring occasionally, until mussels open.
3. Add some of the boiling liquid to a baking dish, then refrigerate the mussels until they are cool enough. Throw away the shells of the mussels you've stored in the fridge.
4. Heat another pan over medium-high heat, add mussels, reserved cooking liquid, chickpeas, and fennel, stir well, and heat them.
5. Add black pepper to taste, lemon juice, and parsley, stir again, divide between plates and serve.

Nutritional Fact:
Calories: 286, Carbohydrates: 49g, Fat: 4g, Protein: 14g, Sodium: 145mg

27. Fish Stew

Preparation Time: 10 mins
Cooking Time: 30 mins
Servings: 4

Ingredients

- 1 avocado, pitted and chopped
- 1 cup chicken stock
- 1 red onion, sliced
- 1 tablespoon oregano, chopped
- 1 tablespoon parsley, chopped
- 1 teaspoon sweet paprika
- 1-pound white fish fillets, boneless, skinless, and cubed
- 2 tablespoons olive oil
- 2 tomatoes, cubed
- A pinch of salt and black pepper
- Juice of 1 lime

Directions:

1. Warm-up oil in a pot over medium heat, add the onion, and sauté within 5 minutes.
2. Toss in the salmon, avocado, and other ingredients, and simmer for another 25 minutes on medium heat.
3. Once done, divide into bowls and serve for dinner.

Nutritional Fact:

Calories: 78, Carbohydrates: 8g, Fat: 1g, Protein: 11g, Sodium: 151 mg

28. Chunky Tomatoes

Preparation Time: 15 mins
Cooking Time: 15 mins
Servings: 3

Ingredients

- ¼ teaspoon chili pepper, chopped
- ½ cup onion, diced
- ½ teaspoon garlic, diced
- 1 teaspoon canola oil
- 1 teaspoon Italian seasonings
- 6 cups plum tomatoes, roughly chopped

Direction:

1. Heat canola oil in the saucepan. Add chili pepper and onion. Cook the vegetables for 5 minutes.
2. Stir them from time to time. After this, add tomatoes, garlic, and Italian seasonings. Close the lid and sauté the dish for 10 minutes.

Nutritional Fact:

Calories 550, Protein 1.7g, Sodium 17mg, Carbohydrates 8.4g, Fat 2.3g

29.   Lemon & Herb Grilled Chicken

Preparation time: 10 mins
Cooking time: 15 mins
Servings: 4

Ingredients

- 1 Lemon, sliced
- 1 sprig Bunch of fresh thyme Fresh rosemary
- 1 tsp Dried oregano
- 1 tsp Kosher salt
- 2 tsp Balsamic vinegar
- 2 tsp Honey
- 4 (680g) Boneless, skinless chicken breasts

Direction:

1. Combine the chicken breasts, lemon slices, thyme, rosemary, oregano, honey, balsamic vinegar, and salt in a resealable plastic bag. Seal the bag and coat well.
2. Refrigerate the bag for a minimum of 1 hour, but up to 24 hours. Preheat the grill to medium-high. Remove the chicken from the marinade. Cook for about 6 to 8 minutes on each side, or until the inside temperature is 165F.
3. Rest and serve.

Nutritional Facts

Calories: 209 Fat: 4g Carb: 1g Protein: 38g Sodium: 147mg

30.   Walnuts and Asparagus Delight

Preparation Time: 5 mins
Cooking Time: 5 mins
Servings: 4

Ingredients:

- Sunflower seeds and pepper to taste
- 1 ½ tablespoons olive oil
- ¾ pound asparagus, trimmed
- ¼ cup walnuts, chopped

Directions:

1. Place a skillet over medium heat. Add olive oil and let it heat.
2. Add asparagus, sauté for 5 minutes until browned.
3. Season with sunflower seeds and pepper. Remove heat.
4. Add walnuts and toss. Serve warm!

Nutritional Fact:

Calories: 124, Fat: 12g, Carbohydrates: 2g, Protein: 3g, Sodium: 55mg, Potassium: 113mg.

Fish & Seafood Recipes

31. Salmon Frittata with Cheese and Herbs

Preparation time: 10 mins
Cooking time: 15 mins
Servings: 4

Ingredients:

- 1 chopped medium white onion
- 1 clove of garlic minced
- 2 tbsp. of fresh dill weed chopped
- 2 tbsp. of fresh parsley chopped
- 2 tbsp. of olive oil
- 4 tbsp. of skim-part grated cheddar
- 6 whole eggs
- 8 oz. of salmon diced and baked
- A pinch of freshly ground black pepper

Directions:

1. Preheat your oven at 380°F.
2. In a large-sized mixing bowl, whisk together 6 eggs and pepper.
3. Stir fry garlic and onions for 3 minutes in heated oil in a medium-sized skillet on medium flame. Stir in the fish and dill and cook for another 2 to 3 minutes.
4. Fill a baking dish halfway with the mixture. Over the top, pour the beaten egg mixture and sprinkle the cheddar cheese.
5. In the oven, bake for about 15 minutes.
6. Just before serving, garnish with chopped parsley.

Nutritional Fact:

Calories 217; Fat 12.5g; Carbohydrates 4.7g; Protein 18.8g; Cholesterol 59mg; Sodium 148mg; Potassium 363mg

32.   Citrus-Glazed Salmon with Zucchini Noodles

Preparation Time: 10 mins
Cooking Time: 20 mins
Servings 4

Ingredients:

- 4 (5- to 6-ounce) pieces salmon
- 2 zucchini (about 16 ounces), spiralized
- 1 teaspoon low-sodium soy sauce
- 1 tablespoon fresh parsley, chopped
- 1 tablespoon fresh chives, chopped
- 1 tablespoon extra-virgin olive oil
- 1 cup freshly squeezed orange juice
- ½ teaspoon kosher salt
- ¼ teaspoon freshly ground black pepper

Directions:

1. Preheat the oven to 350°F. Salt and black pepper should be sprinkled on the fish before cooking. Heat the olive oil in a large oven-safe skillet or sauté pan over medium-high heat. Add the salmon, skin-side down, and sear for 5 minutes, or until the skin is golden brown and crispy. Turn the salmon over and transfer to the oven until your desired doneness is reached—about 5 minutes for medium-rare, 7 minutes for medium, and 9 minutes for medium-well. Place the salmon on a cutting board to rest.
2. Place the same pan on the stove over medium-high heat. Add the orange juice and soy sauce to deglaze the pan. Bring to a simmer, scraping up any brown bits, and continue to simmer 5 to 7 minutes, until the liquid is reduced by half to a syrup-like consistency.
3. Place one piece of salmon on each of four dishes, then top each with a serving of zucchini noodles. Pour the orange glaze over the salmon and zucchini noodles. Garnish with the chives and parsley.

Nutritional Fact:
Calories: 280 fats: 13g; Sodium: 255mg; Potassium: 1100mg; Carbohydrates: 11g; Fibers: 1g; Proteins: 30g; Magnesium: 70mg; Calcium: 45mg

33.   Shrimp Skewers with Lime

Preparation time: 15 mins
Cooking time: 5 mins
Servings: 4

Ingredients:

- 1 lime
- 1 tsp. of lemon juice
- 1/2 tsp. of white pepper
- 1-pound of shrimps, peeled

Directions:

1. Make wedges out of the lime.

2. The shrimp should then be seasoned with lemon juice and white pepper.
3. One by one, thread the lime and lime wedges onto the wooden skewers.
4. Preheat your grill at 400 °F.
5. Place the shrimp skewers on the grill and cook for around 3 minutes on each side, or until light pink.

Nutritional Fact:

Calories 141; Fat 1g; Carbohydrates 3.7g; Protein 26g; Cholesterol 239mg; Sodium 277mg; Potassium 214mg

34. Easy Shrimp and Mango

Preparation Time: 10 mins
Cooking Time: 0 mins
Servings: 4

Ingredients:

- 6 tablespoons avocado mayonnaise
- 3 tablespoons parsley, finely chopped
- 3 tablespoons coconut sugar
- 3 tablespoons balsamic vinegar
- 3 mangos, peeled and cubed
- 1 pound shrimp, peeled, deveined and cooked

Directions:

1. In a bowl, mix vinegar with sugar and mayo and whisk.
2. In another bowl, combine the mango with the parsley and shrimp, add the mayo mix, toss and serve.
3. Enjoy!

Nutritional Fact:

Calories: 214, Fats: 3g, Fibers: 2g, Carbohydrates: 8g, Proteins: 8g, Sodium: 78mg, Potassium: 89mg.

35. Crab, Zucchini and Watermelon Soup

Preparation Time: 4 hours
Cooking Time: 0 mins
Servings: 4

Ingredients:

- zucchini, chopped
- Black pepper to the taste
- 5 cups watermelon, cubed
- 2 pounds tomatoes
- 2 garlic cloves, minced
- 1/3 cup olive oil
- 1 cup crabmeat
- ¼ cup red wine vinegar
- ¼ cup basil, chopped

Directions:

1. In your food processor, mix tomatoes with basil, vinegar, 4 cups watermelon, garlic, 1/3 cup oil and black pepper to the taste, pulse, pour into a bowl and keep in the fridge for 1 hour.
2. Divide this into bowls, add zucchini, crab and the rest of the watermelon and serve.
3. Enjoy!

Nutritional Fact:
Calories: 231, Fats: 3g, Fibers: 3g, Carbohydrates: 6g, Proteins: 8g, Sodium: 56mg, Potassium: 78mg.

36. Tilapia Broccoli Platter

Preparation Time: 4 mins
Cooking Time: 14 mins
Servings: 2

Ingredients:
- 6 ounces tilapia, frozen
- 1 teaspoon lemon pepper seasoning
- 1 Tablespoon garlic, minced
- 1 Tablespoon almond butter
- 1 cup broccoli florets, fresh

Directions:
1. Preheat your oven to 350 degrees F.
2. Add fish in aluminium foil packets. Arrange broccoli around fish. Sprinkle lemon pepper on top, close the packets and seal. Bake for 14 minutes.
3. Take a bowl and add garlic and almond butter, mix well and keep the mixture on the side.
4. Remove the packet from the oven and transfer it to a platter.
5. Place almond butter on top of the fish and broccoli, serve and enjoy!

Nutritional Fact:
Calories: 362, Fat: 25g, Carbohydrates: 2g, Protein: 29g, Sodium: 167mg, Potassium: 170mg.

37. Balsamic Salmon and Peaches Mix

Preparation Time: 10 mins
Cooking Time: 10 mins
Servings: 4

Ingredients:
- Black pepper to taste
- 4 tablespoons olive oil
- 3 lb. salmon steaks
- 2 red onions, cut into wedges
- 2 peaches cut into wedges
- 1 teaspoon thyme, chopped

- 1 tablespoon ginger, grated
- 1 tablespoon balsamic vinegar

Directions:
1. In a small bowl, combine vinegar with ginger, thyme, 3 tablespoons of olive oil and black pepper and whisk
2. In another bowl, mix onion with peaches, 1 tablespoon of oil and pepper and toss. Season salmon with black pepper, place on preheated grill over medium heat, cook for 5 minutes on each side and divide between plates.
3. Put the peaches and onions on the same grill. Cook for 4 mins on each side, divide next to the salmon, drizzle the vinegar mix and serve.
4. Enjoy!

Nutritional Fact:
Calories: 200, Fats: 2g, Fibers: 2g, Carbohydrates: 3g, Proteins: 2g, Sodium: 59mg, Potassium: 100mg.

38. Salmon with Cinnamon

Preparation Time: 10 mins
Cooking Time: 10 mins
Servings: 4

Ingredients:
- 1 tablespoon cinnamon powder
- 1 tablespoon organic olive oil
- 1 tablespoon Pepper to taste
- 2 salmon fillets, boneless and skin on

Directions:
1. Take a clean cooking pan and place it over medium heat. Add oil and let it heat. Add pepper, cinnamon and stir.
2. Add salmon, skin side up and cook for 5 minutes on both sides.
3. Divide between plates and serve.
4. Enjoy!

Nutritional Fact:
Calories: 220, Fat: 8g, Carbohydrates: 11g, Protein: 8g, Sodium: 145mg, Potassium: 123mg.

Poultry Recipes

39.   Hot Chicken Wings

Preparation Time: 15 mins
Cooking Time: 25 mins
Servings: 4

Ingredients:
- ½ stick margarine
- 1 bottle hot sauce
- 10 - 20 chicken wings
- 10 shakes Tabasco sauce
- 2 Tablespoons cayenne pepper
- 2   Tablespoons   honey

Directions:
1. Warm canola oil in a deep pot. Deep-fry the wings until cooked, approximately 20 minutes.
2. Mix the hot sauce, honey, Tabasco, and cayenne pepper in a medium bowl. Mix well.
3. Place the cooked wings on paper towels. Drain the excess oil. Mix the chicken wings in the sauce until coated evenly.
4. Enjoy!

Nutritional Fact:
Calories: 102, Protein: 23g, Carbohydrates: 55g, Sugars: 0.1g, Fat: 14g, Sodium: 140mg, Potassium: 157mg.

40.   Creamy Chicken Fried Rice

Preparation Time: 15 mins

Cooking Time: 45 mins
Servings: 4

Ingredients:
- 1 ½ cups instant rice
- 1 can condensed cream of chicken soup
- 1 cube instant chicken bouillon
- 1 cup mixed frozen vegetables
- 1 cup of water
- 2 pounds of chicken; white and dark meat (diced into cubes)
- 2 Tablespoons butter or margarine
- Salt and pepper to taste

Directions:
1. Take the vegetables out of the freezer. Set aside. Warm large, deep skillet over medium heat. Add the butter or margarine.
2. Season the chicken with salt and pepper before placing it in the pan. Cook till golden brown on both sides.
3. Then, Remove the chicken, adjust the heat and add the rice.
4. Add the water and bouillon. Cook the rice, then add the chicken and the vegetables. Mix in the soup, then simmer until the vegetables are tender.
5. Serve immediately.

Nutritional Fact:
Calories: 119, Protein: 22g, Carbohydrates: 63g, Fat: 18g, Sodium: 180mg, Potassium: 98mg.

41. Chicken Skillet

Preparation time: 5 mins
Cooking time: 25 mins
Servings: 4

Ingredients:
- 1 cup of chopped asparagus
- 1 tbsp. of olive oil
- 1 tsp. of ground black pepper
- 1/2 tsp. of ground paprika
- 1/4 cup of water
- 4 chicken fillets
- 6 tbsp. of low-fat sour cream

Directions:
1. Slice the chicken fillet and season it with paprika and black pepper.
2. Cook the sliced chicken in the skillet for around 3 minutes on each side after adding the olive oil.
3. Then add the asparagus and low-fat sour cream.
4. Close the cover and add water.
5. Cook the food for around 20 minutes in a skillet.

Nutritional Fact:
Calories 241; Fat 12.6g; Carbohydrates 2g; Protein 29.2g; Cholesterol 93mg; Sodium 92mg; Potassium 311mg

42.   Greek Turkey Burger

Preparation Time: 10 mins
Cooking Time: 10 mins
Serves 4

Ingredients:
- 1 teaspoon kosher salt
- 1 tablespoon fresh oregano, chopped
- 1 tablespoon extra-virgin olive oil
- 1 pound ground turkey
- 1 medium zucchini, grated
- 1 large egg, beaten
- 1 garlic clove, minced
- ¼ teaspoon freshly ground black pepper
- ¼ cup whole-wheat breadcrumbs
- ¼ cup red onion, minced
- ¼ cup crumbled feta cheese

Directions:
1. In a large clean bowl, combine the zucchini, turkey, breadcrumbs, onion, feta cheese, egg, garlic, oregano, salt, and black pepper, and mix well. Shape into 4 equal patties.
2. Heat the olive oil in a large non-stick grill pan or skillet over medium-high heat.
3. Add the burgers to the pan and reduce the heat to medium. The first side is cooked for 5 minutes; the second side is cooked for another 5 minutes.

Nutritional Fact:
Calories: 285; fat: 16g; Sodium: 465mg; Potassium: 415mg; Carbohydrates: 9g; Fibers: 2g; Proteins: 26g; Magnesium: 40mg; Calcium: 90mg

43.   Turkey breast with Coconut and zucchini

Preparation Time: 10 mins
Cooking Time: 30 mins
Servings: 4

Ingredients:
- 1 cup coconut cream
- 1 yellow onion, chopped
- 1 zucchini, sliced
- 1-pound turkey breast, skinless, boneless, and cubed
- 2 garlic cloves, minced
- 2 tablespoons olive oil
- A pinch of sea salt
- black pepper

Directions:

1. In a medium-sized saucepan (clean) heat the olive oil over medium heat and add the onion and garlic. Sauté for 5 minutes.
2. Put the meat in and cook for another 5 minutes.
3. Pour in the other ingredients, mix well and bring to a boil over medium heat. Simmer for another 20 minutes.
4. Serve this for lunch.

Nutritional Fact:

Calories 200, Fats: 4g, Fibers: 2g, Sodium: 111mg, Carbohydrates: 14g, Protein: 7g

44. Turkey Sausage and Mushroom Strata

Preparation time: 15 mins
Cooking time: 20 to 30 mins
Servings: 12

Ingredients

- 1 cup Diced mushroom
- 1/2 cup Chopped green onion
- 1/2 teaspoon Paprika
- 1/2 teaspoon Pepper
- 12 oz. Chopped turkey sausage
- 12 oz. Egg substitute
- 2 cups Milk
- 2 tablespoons Grated parmesan cheese
- 3 Large egg
- 4 oz. Shredded cheddar
- 8 oz. Cubed ciabatta bread

Directions:

1. Preheat the oven to 400F. Arrange the bread cubes flat on a baking pan and toast for approximately 8 minutes. Cook the sausage, occasionally stirring, until fully browned and crumbles.
2. In a bowl, combine salt, pepper, paprika, parmesan cheese, egg substitute, eggs, cheddar cheese, and milk. Add the rest of the fixings and mix.
3. Place the mixture in a baking dish, cover tightly, and place in the refrigerator overnight.
4. Remove the cover from the dish. Bake at 350F until golden brown.
5. Cut into slices to serve.

Nutritional Facts

Calories: 288.2 Fat: 12.4g Carb: 18.2g Protein: 24.3g Sodium: 355mg

45. Cast-Iron Roasted Chicken

Preparation time: 20 mins
Cooking time: 80 mins

Servings: 6

Ingredients

- ½ Lemon
- 1 tbsp Olive oil
- 1 tsp Kosher salt
- 3 Garlic cloves
- 3 sprigs Fresh rosemary
- 4lb (1.8kg) Whole chicken
- Ground black pepper
- Small bunch of fresh thyme

Directions:

1. Preheat the oven to 400F. In the centre of a skillet, place the chicken.
2. Using paper towels, pat the skin dry. Insert the thyme, rosemary, lemon, and garlic into the hollow.
3. Utilize kitchen twine to secure the legs together. Drizzle the olive oil over the chicken and season to taste with salt and pepper.
4. Bake for 75–80 minutes, or until the internal temperature is 165F.
5. Remove the pan from the oven carefully and set it aside to cool slightly before serving.

Nutritional Facts
Calories: 293 Fat: 10g Carb: 0g Protein: 47g Sodium: 153mg

46. Turkey Casserole

Preparation time: 5 mins
Cooking time: 25 mins
Servings: 4

Ingredients:

- 1 cup low-fat sour cream
- 1 cup ground turkey
- 1 cup of chopped broccoli
- 1 chopped jalapeno pepper
- 1 tsp. of olive oil
- 1 tsp. of chili flakes
- 1/4 cup of low-fat cheese, shredded

Directions:

1. Olive oil ingredients should be brushed all over the casserole mould—Preheat the oven to 450 °F.
2. Then combine the ground turkey and chili flakes in a casserole shape that has been prepared. Make a good flattening of the mixture.
3. After that, add broccoli, jalapeño pepper, and low-fat sour cream on the top.
4. Cover the mixture with foil and top with shredded cheese.

Nutritional Fact:
Calories 211; Fat 9.2g; Carbohydrates 8g; Protein 24.3g; Cholesterol 64mg; Sodium 144mg; Potassium 335mg

Red Meat Recipes

47.   Pork and Plum Kebabs

Preparation time: 5 mins
Cooking time: 25 mins
Servings: 4

Ingredients:

- 1 1/2 tsp. of ground cumin
- 1 tbsp. of orange juice
- 1/2 tsp. of ground cinnamon
- 1/4 cup of green onions sliced
- 1/4 cup of raspberry spread
- 1/4 tsp. of garlic powder
- 1/4 tsp. of ground red pepper
- 3 plums or nectarines, pitted and cut into wedges
- 3/4 pound of pork loin chops boneless, trimmed and slice into 1-inch pieces

Directions:

1. Half-fill a large resealable bag with the meat. Combine cumin, garlic powder, cinnamon, and red pepper in a small-sized bowl; pour over pork. To coat the meat in spices, close the bag, then shake it.
2. Combine the fruit paste, green onions, and orange juice in a small-sized bowl and set aside.
3. Ascertain that the grill is prepared for direct grilling. Alternately thread pork and plum slices onto skewers. Grill kabobs on a medium flame for around 12 to 14 minutes, flipping once or till meat is cooked through.
4. Brush the raspberry mixture on often throughout the last 5 minutes of grilling.

Nutritional Fact:

Calories 191; Fat 5g; Carbohydrates 15g; Protein 19g; Cholesterol 175mg; Sodium 196mg; Potassium 729mg

48.   Orange Pork Tenderloin

Preparation time: 5 mins
Cooking time: 25 mins
Servings: 4

Ingredients:
- 1 tbsp. of dried oregano
- 1 tsp. of lime zest, grated
- 1 tsp. of onion powder
- 1-pound of pork tenderloin
- 2 tbsp. of avocado oil

Directions:
1. Dry oregano, onion powder, and lime zest is rubbed into the pork tenderloin.
2. Wrap it in foil after brushing it with avocado oil.
3. Preheat the oven to 450°F and bake the meat for around 25 minutes.
4. Using a sharp knife, cut the cooked meat into portions.

Nutritional Fact:
Calories 177; Fat 5g; Carbohydrates 2g; Protein 30g; Cholesterol 83mg; Sodium 68mg; Potassium 525mg

49.   Lamb Meatballs

Preparation Time: 10 mins
Cooking Time: 20 mins
Servings 4

Ingredients:
- ¼ cup fresh mint, chopped
- ¼ cup shallot, chopped
- ¼ teaspoon ground cinnamon
- ¼ teaspoon red pepper flakes
- ½ teaspoon kosher salt
- 1 large egg, beaten
- 1 garlic clove, chopped
- 1 pound ground lamb
- 1 teaspoon ground coriander
- 1 teaspoon ground cumin
- Olive oil cooking spray

Directions:
1. Preheat the oven to 400°F. Grease a 12-cup muffin tin with olive oil cooking spray.
2. In a large bowl, combine the lamb, mint, shallot, egg, garlic, coriander, cumin, salt, cinnamon, and red pepper flakes; mix well.

3. Form the mix into 12 balls and place one in each cup of the prepared muffin tin. Bake for 20 minutes, or until golden brown.

Nutritional Fact:
Calories: 350; fat: 28g; Sodium: 227mg; Potassium: 312mg; Carbohydrates: 2g; Fibers: 1g; Proteins: 21g; Magnesium: 31mg; Calcium: 42mg

50. Delicious Lamb Curry

Preparation time: 5 mins
Cooking time: 25 mins
Servings: 2

Ingredients:

- 10 oz. of cubed lean lamb
- 1 large finely chopped tomato
- 1 finely chopped onion
- 4 finely chopped garlic cloves
- 2 tbsp. of olive oil
- 1 tbsp. of finely chopped parsley
- 2 tsp. of ground cumin
- 2 cups of low-sodium hot chicken stock
- 2 carrots, chopped into 1/2-inch slices
- 1/2 tsp. of turmeric
- 1/2 tsp. of ground coriander

Directions:

1. Heat the oil in a large-sized saucepan on a medium-high flame.
2. When the put is hot, add the lamb and brown it all over. This should only take around 5 minutes.
3. After adding the onion and finely sliced garlic, cook for around 3 minutes.
4. Then, add the carrots, ground cumin, hot chicken stock, turmeric, and ground coriander. Bring everything to a boil.
5. Reduce the flame to low and cook for around 15 minutes, covered. After adding the chopped tomato and parsley, cook for another 2 minutes.
6. Season with black pepper to taste. Enjoy

Nutritional Fact:
Calories 606; Fat 36g; Carbohydrates 12g; Protein 31.6g; Cholesterol 99mg; Sodium 138mg; Potassium 599mg

51. Bistro Beef Tenderloin

Preparation Time: 10 mins
Cooking Time: 45 mins
Servings: 12

Ingredients:

- 1 tsp. kosher salt
- 1/2 tsp. freshly ground pepper

- 2 tbsps. Dijon mustard
- 2 tbsps. extra-virgin olive oil
- 2/3 c. chopped mixed fresh herbs
- 3 lbs. trimmed beef tenderloin

Directions:
1. Preheat oven to 400F.
2. Tie kitchen twine around the loin at three points so that it does not get flattened while grilling.
3. Rub the tenderloin with oil; pat on salt and pepper. Place in a large roasting pan.
4. When a thermometer put into the thickest section of tenderloin reaches 140F for medium-rare, roast for 45 minutes, flipping two or three times throughout roasting to achieve equal cooking.
5. Allow to rest for ten minutes on a chopping board. Remove the string.
6. Place herbs on a large plate. Coat the tenderloin evenly with mustard; then roll in the herbs, pressing gently to adhere. Slice and serve.

Nutritional Fact:
Calories: 280, Fats: 20.6g, Carbohydrates: 0.9g, Proteins: 22.2g, Sugars: 0g, Sodium: 160mg, Potassium: 64mg.

52.   Beef and Broccoli with Oyster Flavour

Preparation time: 5 mins
Cooking time: 25 mins
Servings: 4

Ingredients:
- 1 1/2 pounds of sirloin beef, cut into strips
- 1 head of broccoli, cut into small florets
- 1/4 cup of low-sodium oyster sauce
- 1/4 cup of water
- 2 minced cloves of garlic
- 2 tbsp. of olive oil
- 2 thinly sliced shallots
- Freshly ground black pepper

Directions:
1. In a skillet, heat 2 tbsp. of olive oil on medium flame and stir fry the garlic and shallots for three minutes.
2. Cook for around 5 minutes, or till the beef strips in the skillet are lightly browned.
3. Stir in the broccoli and oyster sauce for another 3 minutes. With the lid on, cook for around 10 minutes.
4. To taste, season with black pepper and serve.

Nutritional Fact:
Calories 295; Fats: 11g; Carbohydrates: 14g; Protein 33.6g; Cholesterol: 36.3mg; Sodium: 121mg; Potassium 563mg

53. Mediterranean Chimichurri Skirt Steak

Preparation Time: 10 mins, plus 30 mins to Marinate
Cooking Time: 15 mins
Servings 4

Ingredients:

- ⅓ cup lemon juice
- ½ teaspoon kosher salt
- ½ teaspoon red pepper flakes
- ⅔ cup extra-virgin olive oil
- ¾ cup fresh mint
- ¾ cup fresh parsley
- 1 to 1½ pounds skirt steak, cut in half if longer than grill pan
- 2 tablespoons dried oregano
- 4 garlic cloves, peeled
- Zest of 1 lemon

Directions:

1. In a food processor or blender, add the mint, parsley, olive oil, lemon juice, lemon zest, oregano, garlic, red pepper flakes, and salt. Process until the mixture reaches your desired consistency—anywhere from a slightly chunky to smooth purée. Remove a half cup of the chimichurri mixture and set aside.
2. Pour the remaining chimichurri mixture into a medium bowl or zip-top bag and add the steak. Mix together well and marinate for at least 30 minutes, and up to 8 hours in the refrigerator.
3. In a grill pan over medium-high heat, add the steak and cook 4 minutes on each side (for medium rare). Cook an additional 1 to 2 minutes per side for medium.
4. Place the steak on a cutting board, tent with foil to keep it warm, and let it rest for 10 minutes. Thinly slice the steak crosswise against the grain and serve with the reserved sauce.

Nutritional Fact:
Calories: 460; fat: 38g; Sodium: 241mg; Potassium: 505mg; Carbohydrates: 5g; Fibers: 2g; Proteins: 28g; Magnesium: 45mg; Calcium: 65mg

54. Tarragon Pork Steak with Tomatoes

Preparation Time: 10 mins
Cooking Time: 22 mins
Servings: 4

Ingredients:

- 1 tablespoon olive oil
- 4 medium pork steaks
- 8 cherry tomatoes, halved
- A handful of tarragon, chopped
- Black pepper to the taste

Directions:

1. Heat a pan with the oil over medium-high flame.
2. Add steaks, season with black pepper, cook them for 6 minutes on each side and divide between plates.
3. Heat the same pan over medium flame.

4. Add the tomatoes and the tarragon, cook for 10 minutes, divide next to the pork and serve.
5. Enjoy!

Nutritional Fact:
Calories: 263, Fats: 14g, Fibers: 6g, Carbohydrates: 12g, Proteins: 16g, Sodium: 59mg, Potassium: 198mg.

Vegetables Recipes

55. Lentil Quinoa Gratin with Butternut Squash

Preparation Time: 15 mins
Cooking Time: 1 hour and 15 mins
Servings: 3

Ingredients:
For the Lentils and Squash:
- ¼ cup diced shallot
- ¼ cup low-fat milk
- ½ cup dried green or red lentils, rinsed
- ½ cup quinoa
- 1 teaspoon chopped fresh rosemary
- 1 teaspoon olive oil, divided

For the Gratin Topping:
- ¼ cup panko breadcrumbs
- 1 teaspoon olive oil
- 1/3 cup shredded Gruyere cheese

- 2 cups frozen cubed butternut squash
- 2 cups of water
- Freshly ground black pepper
- Non-stick cooking spray
- Pinch salt

Directions:
1. Preheat the oven to 400°F. Grease a 1½-quart casserole dish or an 8-by-8-inch baking dish with cooking spray.
2. In a medium saucepan, stir the water, lentils, and salt and boil over medium-high heat. Lower the heat once the water is boiling. Cook for 20 to 25 minutes, then remove the lid and let it rest for 10 minutes. After that, just drain and put aside the lentils in a big basin.

3. 12 teaspoons of oil may be heated in the same pan by placing it over medium heat. A minute of fast stirring will roast the quinoa just enough. Cook for approximately 20 minutes, according to the instructions on the box.
4. Meanwhile, heat the remaining olive oil in a medium pan over low heat while the quinoa is cooking. In approximately 3 minutes, add the shallots and cook them until they are transparent. Cook for 1–2 minutes with the butternut squash, milk, and thyme.
5. Remove, and then transfer to the lentil bowl. Toss in the quinoa, being careful not to overcook it. Season with pepper to taste. Transfer the mixture to the casserole dish.
6. For the gratin topping, mix the panko breadcrumbs with the olive oil in a small bowl. Put the breadcrumbs over the casserole and top them with the cheese. Bake the casserole for 25 minutes and serve.

Nutritional Fact:
Calories: 576, Fats: 15g, Carbohydrates: 87g, Fibers: 12g, Proteins: 28g, Sodium: 329mg, Potassium: 1176mg.

56. Vegan Tomato and Peanut Stew

Preparation time: 5 mins
Cooking time: 25 mins
Servings: 4

Ingredients:
- Onion powder to taste
- Ground cayenne pepper to taste
- Garlic powder to taste
- 6 chopped cloves of garlic
- 4 coarsely chopped large tomatoes
- 2 diced green bell peppers
- 1/3 cup of crushed peanuts
- 1/2 chopped red onion
- 1 tbsp. of vegetable oil
- 1 finely chopped small onion
- 1 1/2 cups of water

Directions:
1. In a medium-sized cooking saucepan, heat the oil on medium flame.
2. Introduce the red and white onion, bell pepper, garlic, and peanuts and cook for about 2 to 3 minutes with.
3. Bring to a boil with the tomatoes, water, onion powder, garlic powder, and cayenne pepper.
4. Reduce the flame to lower the heat, then cook for at least 30 minutes; 1 1/2 hours is ideal.

Nutritional Fact:
Calories 134; Fat 8g; Carbohydrates 14g; Protein 4.6g; Cholesterol 0mg; Sodium 23mg; Potassium 512.3mg

57.   Cauliflower Mashed Potatoes

Preparation Time: 10 mins
Cooking Time: 10 mins
Servings: 4

Ingredients:
- ¼ teaspoon salt
- 1 tablespoon olive oil
- 1/8 teaspoon freshly ground black pepper
- 16 cups water (enough to cover cauliflower)
- 2 teaspoons dried parsley
- 3 pounds cauliflower (1 head), trimmed and cut into florets
- 4 garlic cloves

Directions:
1. Boil a large pot of water, then introduce the cauliflower and garlic. Cook within 10 minutes, then strain.
2. Move it back to the hot pan, and let it stand within 2 to 3 minutes with the lid on.
3. Put the cauliflower plus garlic in a food processor or blender. Add the olive oil, salt, pepper, and purée until smooth. Taste and adjust the salt and pepper.
4. Remove, then put the parsley, and mix until combined. Garnish with additional olive oil, if desired. Serve immediately.

Nutritional Fact:
Calories: 87g, Fat: 4g, Sodium: 210mg, Carbohydrates: 12g, Protein: 4g, Potassium: 67mg.

58.   Butternut-Squash Macaroni and Cheese

Preparation Time: 15 mins
Cooking Time: 20 mins
Servings: 2

Ingredients:
- ¼ cup shredded low-fat cheddar cheese
- 1 cup non-fat or low-fat milk, divided
- 1 cup whole-wheat ziti macaroni
- 1 tablespoon olive oil
- 1 teaspoon Dijon mustard
- 2 cups peeled and cubed butternut squash
- Freshly ground black pepper

Directions:
1. Cook the pasta al dente. Put the butternut squash plus ½ cup milk in a medium saucepan and place over medium-high heat.
2. Season with black pepper. Bring it to a simmer. Lower the heat, then cook until fork-tender, 8 to 10 minutes.
3. To a blender, add squash and Dijon mustard. Purée until smooth.

4. Olive oil should be added to a big sauté pan that is heated to medium-high heat. Add the squash purée and the remaining ½ cup of milk. Simmer within 5 minutes. Add the cheese and stir to combine.
5. Add the pasta to the sauté pan and stir to combine. Serve immediately.

Nutritional Fact:

Calories: 373, Fat: 10g, Sodium: 193mg, Carbohydrates: 59g, Protein: 14g, Potassium: 56mg.

59. Stir-Fry Sesame

Preparation time: 10 mins
Cooking time: 20 mins
Servings: 4

Ingredients:

- 1 bunch of broccolis around 1 pound
- 1 tbsp. of vegetable oil
- 1 tsp. of fresh ginger finely chopped

For the sauce:

- 1 tbsp. of brown sugar
- 1 tbsp. of low-sodium soy sauce
- 1 tbsp. of water

- 3 cloves of minced garlic
- Toasted sesame seeds for garnish optional

- 1 tsp. of toasted sesame oil
- 1/4 tsp. of chili flakes

Directions:

1. Broccoli should be cut into florets. Cut the broccoli stalk into 1" pieces after peeling off the rough outer covering.
2. Set aside the sauce ingredients in a small-sized dish.
3. In a skillet on a medium-high flame, heat the oil and add the broccoli. Cook for around two minutes. Continue to cook for another 2 minutes, or until all the water has evaporated from the pan.
4. Cook, constantly stirring, till the garlic and ginger are fragrant, approximately 1 minute.
5. Cook for a further 2 minutes, or till the sauce mixture is heated through. Serve with sesame seeds sprinkled over the top.

Nutritional Fact:

Calories 99; Fat 5g; Carbohydrates 12g; Protein 5g; Cholesterol 1mg; Sodium 200mg; Potassium 504mg

60. Grilled Veggies with Balsamic

Preparation time: 15 mins
Cooking time: 10 mins
Servings: 4

Ingredients:

- 2 tbsp. of low-sodium soy sauce
- 2 tbsp. of balsamic vinegar
- 3 medium zucchinis, cut into 1/2-inch slices
- 2 medium eggplants, make 1/2-inch slices
- 2 medium green bell peppers, cut into 1/2-inch slices
- 1/2 cup of olive oil
- 1/2 tsp. of ground black pepper

Directions:

1. In a large-sized mixing bowl, combine the olive oil, balsamic vinegar, soy sauce, and pepper. Toss the eggplants, zucchini, and bell peppers with the soy sauce marinade. Allow 45 minutes to marinate.
2. Preheat a clean grill to medium heat and brush the grate liberally with oil. Shake off any extra marinade from the veggies.
3. Grill veggies until cooked, around 10 to 15 minutes on a hot grill, basting with marinade.
4. Serve the cooked veggies with any leftover marinade on a dish.

Nutritional Fact:

Calories 142; Fat 13g; Carbohydrates 5g; Protein 1.4g; Cholesterol 2mg; Sodium 154mg; Potassium 380mg

61. Cauliflower and Potatoes in Coconut Milk

Preparation time: 5 mins
Cooking time: 25 mins
Servings: 4

Ingredients:

- A pinch of freshly ground black pepper
- 7 oz. of new potatoes
- 2 tbsp. of olive oil
- 2 tbsp. of chopped fresh cilantro
- 1/2 cup of water
- 1/2 can of coconut milk (14 oz.)
- 1 tsp. of ground turmeric
- 1 head of cauliflower, florets
- 1 chopped onion

Directions:

1. In a medium-sized cooking saucepan, heat the olive oil and sauté the onion till tender and translucent, approximately 5 minutes.
2. Bring the potatoes and water to a boil. Cover it and cook for about 10 minutes, or till potatoes are nearly soft.
3. Stir the coconut milk, cauliflower, and turmeric into the saucepan, cover, and cook on a low flame for approximately 10 minutes, or till the cauliflower is tender.
4. Remove the cover and season with black pepper before adding the cilantro.

Nutritional Fact:

Calories 244; Fat 17.5g; Carbohydrates 20g; Protein 5.2g; Cholesterol 0mg; Sodium 94.2mg; Potassium 814.1mg

62. Pasta with Tomatoes and Peas

Preparation Time: 15 mins
Cooking Time: 15 mins
Servings: 2

Ingredients:

- ¼ cup grated Parmesan cheese (low-sodium)
- ¼ teaspoon freshly ground black pepper
- ½ cup whole-grain pasta
- 1 cup cherry tomatoes, halved
- 1 cup frozen peas
- 1 tablespoon olive oil
- 1 teaspoon dried basil
- 8 cups water, plus ¼ for finishing

Directions:

1. Cook the pasta al dente. Add the water to the same pot you used to cook the pasta, and when it's boiling, add the peas. Cook within 5 minutes. Drain and set aside.
2. Heat the oil in a large skillet over medium heat. Add the cherry tomatoes, put a lid on the skillet and let the tomatoes soften for about 5 minutes, stirring a few times.
3. Season with black pepper and basil. Toss in the pasta, peas, and ¼ cup of water, stir and remove from the heat. Serve topped with Parmesan.

Nutritional Fact:

Calories: 266, Fat: 12g, Sodium: 320mg, Carbohydrates: 30g, Protein: 13g, Potassium: 67mg.

Soups Recipes

63. Ground Beef Soup

Preparation Time: 10 mins
Cooking Time: 30 mins
Servings: 4

Ingredients:

- ½ cup onion, chopped
- 1 cup beef broth
- 1 tablespoon sour cream
- 1/3 cup white rice, uncooked
- 1-pound lean ground beef
- 2 cups of water
- 2 teaspoons lemon-pepper seasoning blend
- 3 cups of frozen mixed vegetables

Directions:

1. Spray a saucepan with cooking oil and place it over medium heat.
2. Toss in onion and ground beef, then sauté until brown. Stir in broth and the rest of the ingredients, then boil it.
3. Reduce heat to a simmer, then cover the soup to cook for 30 minutes. Garnish with sour cream. Enjoy.

Nutritional Fact:
Calories: 223, Protein: 20g, Fat: 20g, Sodium: 56mg, Potassium: 88mg.

64. Mediterranean Lentil Soup

Preparation Time: 9 mins
Cooking Time: 20 mins
Servings: 4

Ingredients:

- 1 medium yellow or red onion
- 1 tablespoon olive oil
- 1/2 cup red lentils
- 1/2 teaspoon dried parsley
- 1/2 teaspoon ground coriander
- 1/2 teaspoon ground cumin
- 1/2 teaspoon ground sumac
- 1/2 teaspoon red chili flakes
- 2 garlic cloves
- 2 cups water
- 3/4 teaspoons dried mint flakes
- juice of 1/2 lime

Directions:

1. Preheat oil in your Instant Pot on Sauté mode.
2. Add onion and sauté until it turns golden brown. Toss in the garlic, parsley sugar, mint flakes, red chili flakes, sumac, coriander, and cumin.
3. Stir cook this mixture for 2 minutes. Add water, lentils, salt, and pepper. Stir gently.
4. Seal and lock the Instant Pot lid and select Manual mode for 8 minutes at high pressure.
5. Once done, release the pressure completely, then remove the lid. Stir well and add lime juice.

Nutritional Fact:
Calories: 525, Protein: 30g, Fat: 19.3g, Sodium: 76mg, Potassium: 75mg.

65. White Bean Soup

Preparation Time: 13 mins
Cooking Time: 17 mins
Servings: 6

Ingredients:

- 1 cup white beans
- 2 onions, finely chopped
- 1 red bell pepper, chopped
- 1 tsp paprika
- 3 tbsp sunflower oil
- 1-2 tomatoes, grated
- 2-3 carrots
- 4-5 springs of fresh mint and parsley

Directions:

1. Submerge beans in cold water for 3-4 hours, drain and discard the water.
2. Cover the beans with cold water. Add the oil, finely chopped carrots, onions and bell pepper. Boil and simmer until tender.
3. Add the grated tomatoes, mint, paprika and salt. Simmer for another 15 minutes.
4. Serve sprinkled with finely chopped parsley.

Nutritional Fact:
Calories: 210, Fat: 11g, Protein: 5g, Sodium: 185mg, Potassium: 164mg.

66.   Fruit Shrimp Soup

Preparation Time: 10 mins
Cooking Time: 25 mins
Servings: 6

Ingredients

- Bell pepper - 1/2, cubed
- Chicken stock - 6 cup
- Cilantro - 1/3 cup, chopped
- Fish sauce - 2 tablespoons
- Jalapenos - 2, chopped
- Lime juice - 1/4 cup
- Lime leaves - 4
- Pineapple - 1 and 1/2 cups, chopped
- Scallions - 2, sliced
- Shiitake mushroom caps - 1 cup, chopped
- Shrimp - 8 oz., peeled and deveined
- Small ginger pieces - 2, grated
- Stalk lemongrass - 1, smashed
- Sugar - 1 teaspoon
- Tomato - 1, chopped

Direction

1. In a medium saucepan, combine ginger, lemongrass, stock, jalapenos, and lime leaves; stir, bring to a boil over medium heat, and cook for 15 minutes. Reserve the solids.
2. Return the broth to your pot, stir in the pineapple, tomato, mushrooms, bell pepper, sugar, and fish sauce, and cook for 5 minutes over medium heat. Cook for an additional 3 minutes.
3. Remove from the heat. Whisk in the lime juice, cilantro, and scallions. Ladle the soup into soup bowls and serve.

Nutritional Facts
Calories: 290 Fat: 12g Carb: 39g Protein: 7g Sodium: 21mg

67.   Mint Avocado Chilled Soup

Preparation Time: 6 mins
Cooking Time: 0 mins
Servings: 2

Ingredients:

- Salt to taste
- 20 fresh mint leaves
- 1 tablespoon lime juice
- 1 medium ripe avocado
- 1 cup coconut milk, chilled

Directions:
1. Put all the ingredients into an immersion blender and blend until a thick mixture is formed.
2. Allow to cool for 10 minutes and serve chilled.

Nutritional Fact:
Calories: 286, Fats: 27g, Proteins 4.2g, Sodium: 154mg, Potassium: 187mg.

68. Purple Potato Soup

Preparation time: 10 mins
Cooking time: 1 hour and 15 mins
Servings: 6

Ingredients:

- tablespoon thyme, chopped
- Chopped shallots
- Black pepper to the taste
- 6 chopped purple potatoes
- 4 garlic cloves, minced
- 4 cups chicken stock, low-sodium
- 3 tablespoons olive oil
- 1 yellow onion, chopped
- 1 chopped leek
- 1 cauliflower head, florets separated

Directions:
1. In a baking dish, mix potatoes with onion, cauliflower, garlic, pepper, thyme, and half of the oil,
2. Toss to coat, introduce in the oven and bake for 45 minutes at 400 degrees F.
3. Heat the pot with the rest of the oil over medium-high heat, add leeks and shallots, stir and cook for 10 minutes.
4. Add roasted veggies and stock, stir, cook for 20 minutes.
5. Transfer soup to your food processor, blend well, divide into bowls, and serve.

Nutritional Info
Calories: 70 Carbohydrates: 15g Fat: 0g Protein: 2g Sodium 6 mg

69. Mussels and Chickpea Soup

Preparation Time: 10 mins
Cooking Time:10 mins
Servings: 6

Ingredients:

- 1 and ½ tablespoons fresh mussels, scrubbed
- 1 cup chickpeas, rinsed
- 1 cup white wine
- 1 small fennel bulb, sliced

- 2 tablespoons olive oil
- 3 garlic cloves, minced
- 3 tablespoons parsley, chopped
- A pinch of chili flakes
- Black pepper to the taste
- Juice of 1 lemon

Direction:
1. Using a medium-high heat, sauté the garlic and chili flakes in a large skillet with olive oil for a few minutes.
2. Cook for 3-4 minutes, stirring occasionally, until mussels open.
3. Add some of the boiling liquid to a baking dish, then refrigerate the mussels until they are cool enough. Throw away the shells of the mussels you've stored in the fridge.
4. Heat another pan over medium-high heat, add mussels, reserved cooking liquid, chickpeas, and fennel, stir well, and heat them.
5. Add black pepper to taste, lemon juice, and parsley, stir again, divide between plates and serve.

Nutritional Info
Calories: 286, Carbohydrates: 49g, Fat: 4g, Protein: 14g, Sodium: 140 mg

70. Spinach Soup

Preparation Time: 10 mins
Cooking Time: 21 mins
Servings: 6

Ingredients:
- 1 carrot
- 1 large onion
- 1/4 cup white rice
- 1-2 cloves garlic, crushed
- 14 oz frozen spinach
- 3-4 tbsp olive oil
- 4 cups water

Directions:
1. Cook oil in a cooking pot, stir in onion and carrot and sauté together for a few minutes until just softened.
2. Add chopped garlic and rice and stir for a minute.
3. Remove from heat. Add in the chopped spinach along with about 2 cups of hot water and season with salt and pepper.
4. Bring back to a boil, then reduce the heat and simmer for around 30 minutes.

Nutritional Fact:
Calories: 291, Fat: 16g, Protein: 7g, Sodium: 120mg, Potassium: 154mg.

Salad Recipes

71. Cauliflower Lunch Salad

Preparation time: 10 mins
Cooking time: 10 mins
Servings: 4

Ingredients:

- ¼ cup red onion, chopped
- 1 red bell pepper, chopped
- 1 tablespoon cilantro, chopped
- 1 teaspoon mint, chopped
- 1/3 cup low-sodium veggie stock
- 2 cup kalamata olives halved
- 2 tablespoons olive oil
- 6 cups cauliflower florets, grated
- Black pepper to the taste
- Juice of ½ lemon

Direction:

1. Heat-up a pan with the oil over medium-high heat, add cauliflower, pepper and stock, stir, cook within 10 minutes
2. 2Transfer to a container, and keep in the fridge for 2 hours.
3. 3Mix cauliflower with olives, onion, bell pepper, black pepper, mint, cilantro, and lemon juice, toss to coat, and serve.

Nutritional Fact:

Calories: 102, Sodium 97 mg, carbohydrates: 3g, Fat: 10g, Protein: 0g

72.   Quinoa and Scallops Salad

Preparation Time:10 mins
Cooking Time:35 mins
Servings: 6

Ingredients

- ¼ cup cilantro, chopped
- 1 and ½ cup quinoa, rinsed
- 1 cup scallions, sliced
- 1 cup snow peas, sliced diagonally
- 1 teaspoon sesame oil
- 1/3 cup red bell pepper, chopped
- 1/3 cup rice vinegar
- 12 ounces dry sea scallops
- 2 teaspoons canola oil
- 2 teaspoons garlic, minced
- 4 tablespoons canola oil
- 4 teaspoons low sodium soy sauce

Direction:

1. In a clean bowl, mix 2 teaspoons soy sauce with scallops, stir gently, and leave aside for now. Heat a pan with 1 tablespoon canola oil over medium- high heat, add the quinoa, stir and cook for 8 minutes. Put garlic, stir and cook within 1 more minute.
2. Cover and simmer for 15 minutes with the water boiling over medium heat. Allow to cool for five minutes after removing from heat. Cook for an additional 5 mins after adding snow peas.
3. Add 2 t. soy sauce, vinegar, and sesame oil to 3 t. canola oil in a separate bowl. Stir in the quinoa and snow peas, then serve. Stir in the scallions and bell peppers.
4. Remove the scallops from the marinade and pat them dry. Cook the scallops for 1 minute on each side in a hot skillet with 2 tablespoons canola oil. Gently mix them into the quinoa salad, then garnish with chopped cilantro.

Nutritional Fact:
Calories: 181, Carbohydrates: 12g, Fat: 6g, Protein: 13g, Sodium: 153 mg

73.   Fruited Quinoa Salad

Preparation Time: 15 mins
Cooking Time: 15 mins
Servings: 2

Ingredients

- ¼ cup apple cider vinegar
- ¼ cup olive oil
- ½ cup blueberries
- 1 cup strawberry, quartered
- 1 mango, sliced and peeled
- 1 tablespoon pine nuts Chopped
- 1 teaspoon sugar
- 2 cups cooked quinoa
- 3 tablespoons lemon juice
- mint leave for garnish Lemon vinaigrette:

- Zest 1 lemon

Direction:
1. For the Lemon Vinaigrette, whisk olive oil, apple cider vinegar, lemon zest and juice, and sugar to a container; set aside.
2. Combine quinoa, mango strawberries, blueberries, and pine nuts in a large container.
3. Stir the lemon vinaigrette and garnish with mint.
4. Serve and enjoy!

Nutritional Fact
Calories 425, Sodium 16mg, Carbohydrates 76.1g, Proteins 11.3g, Fat 10.9

74.   Orange Celery Salad

Preparation Time: 16 mins
Cooking Time: 0 mins
Servings: 6

Ingredients:
- ¼ cup red onion, sliced
- ¼ teaspoon black pepper
- ¼ teaspoon sea salt, fine
- ½ cup green olives
- 1 tablespoon lemon juice, fresh
- 1 tablespoon olive brine
- 1 tablespoon olive oil
- 2 oranges, peeled & sliced
- 3 celery stalks, sliced diagonally in ½ inch slices

Directions:
1. Put your oranges, olives, onion and celery in a shallow bowl.
2. Stir oil, olive brine and lemon juice, pour this over your salad.
3. Season with salt and pepper before serving.

Nutritional Fact:
Calories: 65, Protein: 2g, Fat: 0.2g, Sodium: 43mg, Potassium: 123mg.

75.   Roasted Eggplant Salad

Preparation Time: 14 mins
Cooking Time: 36 mins
Servings: 6

Ingredients:
- 1 red onion, sliced
- 1 teaspoon basil

- 1 teaspoon oregano
- 1 teaspoon thyme
- 2 cups cherry tomatoes
- 2 tablespoons parsley
- 3 eggplants, peeled and cubed
- 3 tablespoons olive oil

Directions:
1. Start by heating your oven to 350F. Season your eggplant with basil, salt, pepper, oregano, thyme and olive oil.
2. Bake it for half an hour on a baking sheet.
3. Toss with your remaining ingredients before serving.

Nutritional Fact:
Calories: 148, Protein: 3.5g, Fat: 7.7g, Sodium: 12mg, Potassium: 45mg.

76. Chickpea and Zucchini Salad

Preparation Time: 10 mins
Cooking Time: 0 mins
Servings: 3

Ingredients:
- ¼ cup balsamic vinegar
- 1 tablespoon of capers, drained and chopped
- ½ cup crumbled feta cheese
- 1 can chickpeas, drained
- 1 garlic clove, chopped
- ½ cup Kalamata olives, chopped
- ½ cup sweet onion, chopped
- ½ tsp oregano
- 1 pinch of red pepper flakes, crushed
- ¾ cup red bell pepper, chopped
- 1 tablespoon chopped rosemary
- 2 cups of zucchini, diced
- Salt and pepper to taste
- 1/3 cup chopped basil leaves
- 1/3 cup of olive oil

Directions:
1. Combine the vegetables in a bowl and cover well.
2. Serve at room temperature.
3. But for best results, refrigerate the bowl for a few hours before serving to allow the flavours to blend.

Nutritional Fact:
Calories: 258, Fat: 12g, Carbohydrates: 19g, Protein: 5.6g, Sodium: 54mg, Potassium: 29mg.

77.   Mediterranean Potato Salad

Preparation Time: 15 mins
Cooking Time: 10 mins
Servings: 2

Ingredients:
- 1 bunch of basil leaves, torn
- 1 can of cherry tomatoes
- 1 garlic clove, crushed
- 1 onion, sliced
- 1 tablespoon of olive oil
- 1 teaspoon of oregano
- 100 g of roasted red pepper. Slices
- 300g potatoes, cut in half
- salt and pepper to taste

Directions:
1. Sauté the onions in a saucepan. Add oregano and garlic. Then cooks everything for one minute.
2. Add the pepper and tomatoes. Season well, and simmer for about 10 minutes. Put that aside.
3. In a saucepan, boil the potatoes in salted water. Cook until tender, about 15 minutes. Drain well.
4. Mix the potatoes with the sauce and add the basil and olives. Finally, throw everything away before serving.

Nutritional Fact:
Calories: 111, Fat: 9g, Carbohydrates: 16g, Protein: 3g, Sodium: 59mg, Potassium: 75mg.

78.   Cucumber Chicken Salad with Spicy Peanut Dressing

Preparation Time: 15 mins
Cooking Time: 0 mins
Servings: 2

Ingredients:
- 1 cooked chicken fillet, grated into thin strips
- 1 cucumber with peeled and cut into thin strips
- 1 tablespoon chili paste
- 1 tablespoon low-sodium soy sauce
- 1 teaspoon grilled sesame oil
- 1/2 cup peanut butter
- 2 tablespoons chopped peanuts
- 4 tablespoons of water, or more if necessary

Directions:
1. Combine peanut butter, soy sauce, sesame oil, chili paste, and water in a bowl.
2. Place the cucumber slices on a dish. Garnish with grated chicken and sprinkle with sauce.
3. Sprinkle the chopped peanuts and serve.

Nutritional Fact:
Calories: 720, Fat: 54g, Carbohydrates: 8.9g, Protein: 45.9g, Sodium: 54mg, Potassium: 95mg.

Sauces and Dressings Recipes

79.   Herb And Feta Dip

Preparation time: 10 mins
Cooking time: 0 mins
Servings: 4

Ingredients:

- 1 cup of rinsed white beans
- 1 tbsp. of lemon juice
- 1 tsp. of freshly ground pepper
- 1/2 cup of feta cheese crumbled
- 1/4 cup of fresh chives chopped
- 1/4 cup of fresh mint chopped
- 1/4 cup of fresh parsley chopped
- 1/4 cup of fresh dill chopped
- 3/4 cup of plain yogurt non-fat

Directions:

1. Puree the beans, feta, yogurt, lemon juice, and pepper in a food processor till smooth.
2. Add the herbs and purée till they are completely incorporated.
3. Place in the refrigerator till ready to eat.

Nutritional Fact:
Calories 68; Fat 3g; Carbohydrates 9g; Protein 5g; Cholesterol 8.8mg; Sodium 132mg; Potassium 188mg

80.   White Sauce

Preparation time: 5 mins
Cooking time: 10 mins
Servings: 4

Ingredients:

- 1-quart of low-fat milk
- 4 sprigs of chopped fresh thyme
- A pinch of cayenne pepper, or more to taste
- 1/2 cup of unsalted butter
- 1/2 cup of almond flour
- 1/8 tsp. of freshly grated nutmeg

Directions:

1. In a small-sized saucepan, melt the butter on a low flame—Cook for around 5 minutes after adding the flour.
2. Add 1 cup of chilled milk, mix in for 1 minute. Add the second cup of milk and stir for another minute.
3. Stir in the remaining 2 cups of milk, thyme, cayenne pepper, and nutmeg, and cook, occasionally stirring, till the sauce thickens, around 10 minutes.

Nutritional Fact:

Calories 192; Fat 14g; Carbohydrates 6g; Protein 5g; Cholesterol 40.3mg; Sodium 132mg; Potassium 196mg

81.   Basil Tofu Dressing

Preparation time: 10 mins
Cooking time: 0 mins
Servings: 4

Ingredients:

- 1 clove of minced garlic
- 1/2 (12 oz.) package of firm silken tofu
- 1/2 tsp. of Dijon mustard
- 2 tbsp. of apple juice
- 2 tbsp. of cider vinegar
- 2 tbsp. of fresh basil chopped

Directions:

1. Blend tofu, basil, cider vinegar, garlic, apple juice, and Dijon mustard till completely smooth in a blender.

Nutritional Fact:

Calories 38; Fat 2g; Carbohydrates 2g; Protein 4g; Cholesterol 0mg; Sodium 59mg; Potassium 67mg

82.   Cucumber and Tomato Sauce

Prep time: 5 mins
Cooking time: 25 mins
Servings: 4

Ingredients:
- 1 cup of chopped Roma tomatoes
- 1 tsp. of each onion and garlic powder
- 1/2 cup of chopped red bell pepper
- 1/2 tsp. of black pepper
- 1/2 tsp. of red pepper flakes
- 1/4 cup of olive oil
- 2 cloves of minced garlic
- 2 cups of diced cucumber
- 2 tsp. of dried basil
- 4 1/2 tsp. of stevia

Directions:
1. In a medium-sized cooking saucepan, heat the olive oil. Simmer for a few minutes, till garlic is aromatic, add the dried basil and cook more for the next few seconds.
2. Combine the tomatoes, garlic powder, onion powder, black pepper, red pepper flakes, and sweetener. Stir add the red pepper and cucumber after bringing to a boil.
3. Continue to boil, stirring periodically, for around 10 to 15 minutes, or till the mixture has reduced to a sauce-like consistency.

Nutritional Fact:
Calories 115; Fat 9g; Carbohydrates 8g; Protein 1g; Cholesterol 0mg; Sodium 100mg; Potassium 201mg

83.   Maple Dijon Dressing

Preparation Time: 5 mins
Cooking Time: 0 mins
Servings: 1

Ingredients:
- ¼ cup apple cider vinegar
- ¼ teaspoon black pepper
- 2 tablespoons low-sodium vegetable broth
- 2 tablespoons maple syrup
- 2 teaspoons Dijon mustard

Directions:
1. Mix the apple cider vinegar, Dijon mustard, maple syrup, vegetable broth, and black pepper in a resealable container until well incorporated.
2. The dressing can be refrigerated for up to 5 days.

Nutritional Fact:
Calories: 82, Fats: 0.3g, Carbohydrates: 19.3g, Proteins: 0.6g, Fibers: 0.7g, Sodium: 53mg, Potassium: 67mg.

84. Cilantro-Peanut Dipping Sauce

Preparation time: 5 mins
Cooking time: 25 mins
Servings: 4

Ingredients:

- 10 sprigs of finely chopped cilantro leave
- 4 cloves of minced garlic, minced
- 2 tsp. of fresh ginger root minced
- 2 tsp. of red pepper flakes crushed
- 1/2 cup of chunky peanut butter
- 1/2 cup of peanut oil
- 1/4 cup of red wine vinegar
- 1/4 cup of lemon juice fresh
- 1/4 cup of low-sodium soy sauce

Directions:

1. In a food processor, combine peanut butter, lemon juice, red wine vinegar, peanut oil, and soy sauce till smooth.
2. Combine the ginger, cilantro, garlic, and red pepper flakes. Blend till the mixture is completely smooth.
3. Refrigerate till ready to serve.

Nutritional Fact:

Calories 114; Fat 11g; Carbohydrates 3g; Protein 2g; Cholesterol 0mg; Sodium 65mg; Potassium 97mg

Snacks Recipes

85. Zucchini Sticks

Preparation Time: 10 mins
Cooking Time: 15 mins
Servings: 6

Ingredients
- ¼ tsp. freshly ground black pepper
- ½ cup No-salt-added pasta sauce
- ½ tsp. garlic powder
- ½ tsp. onion powder
- 1 Egg white
- 1 Tbsp. grated Parmesan cheese
- 1 Tbsp. Water
- 1 tsp. dried Italian seasoning
- 1/8 tsp. ground sweet paprika
- 2 Medium zucchinis, cut into 16 equal wedges
- 3 Tbsp. salt-free breadcrumbs

Direction:
1. Preheat the oven to 450F. Spray a baking sheet with oil.
2. Beat the egg whites and water in a bowl.
3. In another bowl, place breadcrumbs, cheese, and seasonings and whisk to combine.
4. Dip each piece of zucchini in the egg. Then roll in breadcrumbs. Place on the baking sheet and bake for 15 minutes.
5. Meanwhile, warm the pasta sauce on the stovetop. Serve zucchini stick with warm sauce.

Nutritional Fact
Calories: 39, Fat: 1g, Carbohydrates: 6g, Protein: 2g, Sodium 28mg

86.   Oatmeal Cookies

Preparation Time: 15 mins
Cooking Time: 12 mins
Servings: 18

Ingredients

- ¼ cups raisins
- ¼ cups warm filtered water
- ¼ tsp. ground ginger
- ¼ tsp. ground nutmeg
- ½ tsp. baking soda
- ½ tsp. ground cinnamon
- 1 large apple
- 1 tsp. apple cider vinegar
- 2 cups quick oats
- 2 tbsp. cold water
- 2 tsp. chia seeds
- 4 Medjool dates

Direction:

1. Preheat the oven to 375F. Line a large cookie sheet with a large greased parchment paper.
2. In a bowl, mix together warm water and chia seeds. Set aside until thickened.
3. In a large food processor, add 1 cup of the oats and pulse until finely ground. Transfer the ground oats in a large bowl. Add the remaining oats, baking soda, spices and raisins and mix well.
4. Now in the blender, add the remaining ingredients and pulse until smooth. Transfer the apple mixture into the bowl with oat mixture and mix well.
5. Add the chia seeds mixture and stir to combine. Spoon the mixture onto the prepared cookie sheet in a single layer and with your finger, flatten each cookie slightly.
6. Bake until golden brown or for about 12 minutes. Remove from oven and place the cookie sheet onto a wire rack to cool for about 5 minutes. Invert the cookies onto the wire rack to cool before serving.

Nutritional Fact:

Calories: 68, Fat: 0.8g, Carbohydrates: 14.5g, Fibers: 2g, Sugars: 6.6g, Proteins: 1.6g, Sodium: 37mg

87.   Roasted Chickpeas

Preparation Time: 10 mins
Cooking Time: 45 mins
Servings: 12

Ingredients

- ¼ tsp. ground cumin
- ½ tsp. dried oregano, crushed
- ½ tsp. smoked paprika
- 1 tbsp. olive oil
- 2 garlic cloves, minced
- 4 C. cooked chickpeas

Direction:

1. Preheat the oven to 400 °F. Prepare a big baking sheet with non-stick cooking spray and set it aside.
2. Lay the chickpeas out in a single layer on the prepared baking sheet. Toss the chickpeas around every 10 minutes throughout the 30-minute roasting period.
3. Mix garlic, thyme and other spices in a small bowl as you wait. It's time to take out that baking sheet.
4. Toss the chickpeas with the garlic mixture and oil and coat them well, then transfer them to a serving dish. Continue roasting for a further 10 to 15 minutes, depending on the oven.
5. Turn off the oven, but keep the baking pan inside for approximately 10 minutes before serving.

Nutritional Fact

Calories: 92, Sodium: 10mg, Fat: 1.9g, Carbohydrates: 15g, Fibers: 0.1g, Proteins: 4.1g

88. Pumpkin Almond Bites

Preparation time: 15 mins
Cooking time: 0 mins
Servings: 4

Ingredients:

- ½ cup of almond flour
- 1 packet of stevia
- 1/2 cup of gluten-free rolled oats
- 1/2 tsp. of ground cinnamon
- 1/2 tsp. of almond extract
- 1/4 cup of pumpkin puree
- 1/4 cup of almond butter
- 1/4 tsp. of ground cloves
- 1/4 tsp. of ground nutmeg

Directions:

1. In a food processor, combine the oats, almond butter, almond flour, pumpkin puree, stevia sugar replacement, almond extract, cinnamon, cloves, and nutmeg until mixed.
2. Refrigerate for at least 30 minutes after rolling the mixture into balls and arranging them on a dish or baking sheet.

Nutritional Fact:

Calories 158; Fat 11.8g; Carbohydrates 10.2g; Protein 4.8g; Cholesterol 0mg; Sodium 125.5mg; Potassium 127.1mg

89. Spiced Peanut Butter Apples

Preparation time: 5 mins
Cooking time: 25 mins
Servings: 4

Ingredients:

- 1/2 tsp. of vanilla extract
- 1/8 tsp. of ground cardamom
- 1/8 tsp. of ground cloves
- 4 Granny Smith apples
- 6 tbsp. of peanut butter

Directions:
1. Preheat the oven to 350 °F. Using a sharp knife, remove the tops of the apples.
2. Using an apple corer, remove the cores from the apples while keeping the bottoms intact.
3. Fill the cored apples with 1 1/2 tbsp. of peanut butter and a splash of vanilla extract. Sprinkle cardamom and cloves over apples in a baking pan.
4. Bake for around 30 mins in a preheated oven till apples are mellow and aromatic.

Nutritional Fact:

Calories 206; Fat 12.3g; Carbohydrates 20g; Protein 6.5g; Cholesterol 0mg; Sodium 113.6mg; Potassium 312.3mg

90. Crab Cake Lettuce Cups

Preparation Time: 35 mins
Cooking Time: 20 mins
Servings: 4

Ingredients:
- ¼ cup extra-virgin olive oil
- ¼ cup minced red onion
- ½ cup almond flour
- ½ teaspoon freshly ground black pepper
- 1 large egg
- 1 teaspoon celery salt
- 1 teaspoon dried dill (optional)
- 1 teaspoon garlic powder
- 1-pound jumbo lump crab
- 2 tablespoons Dijon mustard
- 2 teaspoons smoked paprika
- 4 large lettuce leaves, thick spine removed
- 6 tablespoons Roasted Garlic Aioli

Directions:
1. Put the crabmeat in a large bowl and pick out any visible shells, then break apart the meat with a fork. In a small bowl, scourge together the egg, 2 tablespoons aioli, and Dijon mustard. Add to the crabmeat and blend with a fork.
2. Add the almond flour, red onion, paprika, celery salt, garlic powder, dill (if using), and pepper and combine well. Allow rest at room temperature for 10 to 15 minutes.
3. Form into 8 small cakes, about 2 inches in diameter. Cook the olive oil over medium-high heat.
4. Fry the cakes until browned, 2 to 3 minutes per side. Wrap, decrease the heat to low and cook for another 6 to 8 minutes, or until set in the centre. Remove from the skillet.
5. To serve, wrap 2 small crab cakes in each lettuce leaf and top with 1 tablespoon aioli.

Nutritional Fact:

Calories: 344, Fat: 24g, Carbohydrates: 2g, Protein: 24g, Sodium: 45mg, Potassium: 123mg.

91.   Cucumbers Filled with Salmon

Preparation Time: 10 mins
Cooking Time: 0 mins
Servings: 4

Ingredients:

- ¼ teaspoon freshly ground black pepper
- ½ teaspoon salt
- 1 (4-ounce) can red salmon
- 1 medium very ripe avocado
- 1 tablespoon extra-virgin olive oil
- 2 large cucumbers, peeled
- 3 tablespoons chopped fresh cilantro
- Zest and juice of 1 lime

Directions:

1. Cut the cucumber into 1-inch-thick wedges and, using a spoon, scrape the seeds from the centre of each wedge and stand it upright on a plate.
2. In a medium bowl, combine the salmon, avocado, olive oil, lime zest and juice, cilantro, salt and pepper and mix until creamy.
3. Scoop the salmon mixture into the centre of each cucumber segment and serve chilled.

Nutritional Fact:

Calories: 159, Fat: 11g, Carbohydrates: 3g, Protein: 9g, Sodium: 65mg, Potassium: 123mg.

92.   Cheese Crackers

Preparation Time: 1 hour and 15 mins
Cooking Time: 15 mins
Servings: 20

Ingredients:

- ¼ teaspoon freshly ground black pepper
- 1 cup almond flour
- 1 cup finely shredded Manchego cheese
- 1 large egg
- 1 teaspoon salt, divided
- 4 tablespoons butter at room temperature

Directions:

1. With an electric mixer, beat the butter and grated cheese until well combined and smooth. Stir in the almond flour with ½ teaspoon salt and pepper.
2. Gradually incorporate the almond flour mixture into the cheese, mixing constantly until the dough comes together to form a ball.
3. Place on a piece of parchment or plastic wrap and roll into a cylindrical log about 1½ inches thick. Seal well and freeze for at least 1 hour. Preheat oven to 350°F. Place parchment paper or silicone baking mats on 2 baking sheets.
4. To make the egg wash, scourge together the egg and remaining ½ teaspoon salt. Slice the refrigerated dough into small rounds, about ¼ inch thick, and place on the lined baking sheets.

5. Egg washes the tops of the crackers and bake until the crackers are golden and crispy. Put on a wire rack to cool. Serve warm or, once fully cooled, store in an airtight container in the refrigerator for up to 1 week.

Nutritional Fact:
Calories: 243, Fat: 23g, Carbohydrates: 1g, Protein: 8g, Sodium: 68mg, Potassium: 123mg.

Desserts Recipes

93. Strawberry Bruschetta

Preparation Time: 15 mins
Cooking Time: 0 mins
Servings: 12

Ingredients:
- 1 cup basil leaves
- 1 loaf sliced Ciabatta bread
- 2 containers of strawberries, sliced
- 5 tablespoons balsamic glaze
- 8 ounces goat cheese

Direction:
1. Wash and slice strawberries; set aside.
2. Rinse and chop the basil leaves; set aside.
3. Slice the ciabatta bread and spread some goat cheese evenly on each slice; add strawberries, balsamic glaze, and top with basil leaves.
4. Serve on a platter.

Nutritional Fact
Calories 80, Sodium 59 mg, Fats 2 g, Proteins 3 g, Carbohydrates 12 g

94. Pumpkin with Chia Seeds Pudding

Preparation Time: 60 mins
Cooking Time: 0 mins
Servings: 4

Ingredients:

For the Pudding:
- ¼ cup raw maple syrup
- ½ cup organic chia seeds
- 1 ¼ cup low-fat milk
- 1 cup pumpkin puree extract

For the Toppings:
- ¼ cup blueberries
- ¼ cup coarsely chopped almonds
- ¼ cup organic sunflower seeds

Direction:
1. Add all the ingredients for the pudding in a bowl and mix until blended.
2. Cover and store in a chiller for 1-hour.
3. Remove from the chiller, transfer contents to a jar and add the ingredients for the toppings.
4. Serve immediately.

Nutritional Fact

Calories: 189 Sodium: 42 mg Fats: 7 g Carbohydrates 27 g Fibers: 4 g Proteins: 5 g Sugar: 18 g

95. Grilled Pineapple Strips

Preparation Time: 15 mins
Cooking Time: 5 mins
Servings: 6

Ingredients:
- 1 Dash of iodized salt
- 1 pineapple
- 1 tablespoon lime juice extract
- 1 tablespoon olive oil
- 1 tablespoon raw honey
- 3 tablespoons brown sugar
- Vegetable oil

Direction:
1. Peel the pineapple, remove the eyes of the fruit, and discard the core.
2. Slice the pineapple lengthwise, forming six wedges.
3. Brush the coating mixture on the pineapple. Grease an oven or outdoor grill rack with vegetable oil.
4. Place the pineapple wedges on the grill rack and heat for a few minutes per side until golden brownish, basting it frequently with a reserved glaze. Serve on a platter.

Nutrition Fact:

Calories: 97 Fats: 2 g Carbohydrates: 20 g Proteins: 1 g Fibers: 1 g Sugars: 17 g Sodium: 2 mg

96. Frozen Mango Treat

Preparation time: 10 mins
Cooking Time: 0 mins
Servings: 4

Ingredients:

- ½ C. chilled water
- 1 tbsp. fresh mint leaves
- 1 tbsp. fresh mint leaves
- 2 tbsp. fresh lime juice
- 3 C. frozen mango, peeled, pitted, and chopped

Direction:

1. In a high-velocity blender, add all ingredients and pulse until smooth.
2. Transfer into serving bowls and serve immediately.

Nutritional Fact:

Calories: 76, Fats: 0.5g, Carbohydrates: 18.7g, Fibers: 2.1g, Sugar: 16.9g, Proteins: 1.1g, Sodium: 3mg

97. Zucchini Muffins

Preparation Time: 15 mins
Cooking Time: 30 mins
Servings: 12

Ingredients:

- ¼ teaspoon ground nutmeg
- ¼ teaspoon iodized salt
- ½ cup of sugar
- ¾ cup skim milk
- 1 cup shredded zucchini
- 1 large egg
- 1 tablespoon baking powder
- 2 cups of all-purpose flour
- 2 teaspoons grated lemon rind
- 3 tablespoons vegetable oil
- Vegetable oil cooking spray

Direction:

1. Mix the flour, baking powder, sugar, salt, plus lemon rinds in a bowl. Create a well in the centre of the flour batter.
2. In another container, mix zucchini, milk, vegetable oil, and egg. Coat muffin cups with vegetable oil cooking spray.
3. Divide the batter equally into 12 muffin cups. Transfer the muffin cups to the baking pan, put it in a microwave oven, and bake at 400 °F within 30 minutes until light golden brown.
4. Remove, then allow to cool on a wire rack before serving.

Nutritional Fact:

Proteins: 0 g, Calories: 169, Sodium: 211.5 mg, Carbohydrates: 29.1 g, Fats: 4.8 g, Fibers: 2.5 g

98.   Grapefruit Compote

Preparation Time: 5 mins
Cooking Time: 8 mins
Servings: 4

Ingredients:
- ½ cup chopped mint
- 1 cup palm sugar
- 2 peeled and cubed grapefruits
- 64 oz. Sugar-free red grapefruit juice

Directions:
1. Take all ingredients and combine them into Instant Pot. Cook on Low for 8 minutes, then divide into bowls and serve!

Nutritional Fact:
Calories: 131, Fats: 1g, Carbohydrates: 12g, Net Carbohydrates: 11g, Proteins: 2g, Fibers: 2g, Sodium: 175mg, Potassium: 198mg.

99.   Dates Brownies

Preparation Time: 10 mins
Cooking Time: 15 mins
Servings: 8

Ingredients:
- ½ teaspoon baking soda
- 1 banana, peeled and chopped
- 1 tablespoon coconut sugar
- 12 dates
- 2 tablespoons cocoa powder
- 28 ounces canned lentils, no-salt-added, rinsed and drained
- 4 tablespoons almond butter

Directions:
1. Put lentils in your food processor. Pulse, add dates, sugar, banana, baking soda, almond butter and cocoa powder. Pulse well.
2. Pour the mix into a lined pan, spread, and bake in the oven at 375 degrees F for 15 minutes. Leave the mix aside to cool down a bit, cut into medium pieces and serve.
3. Enjoy!

Nutritional Fact:
Calories: 202, Fats: 4g, Fibers: 2g, Carbohydrates: 12g, Proteins: 6g, Sodium: 168mg, Potassium: 354mg.

100. Sautéed Bananas with Orange Sauce

Preparation Time: 5 mins
Cooking Time: 5 mins
Servings: 4

Ingredients:

- ¼ c. frozen pure orange juice concentrate
- ¼ c. sliced almonds
- 1 tsp. cinnamon
- 1 tsp. fresh grated ginger
- 1 tsp. orange zest
- 2 tbsps. margarine
- 4 firm, sliced ripe bananas

Directions:

1. Make sure that the margarine is melt over medium heat, but not browning, in a pan.
2. Add the orange zest, cinnamon, and ginger. One minute of stirring before adding the orange juice concentrate.
3. Continually swirl the sauce while it cooks until it reaches a smooth consistency.
4. Stir the bananas into the sauce for 1-2 minutes, until they are warmed through and well-coated with the sauce.
5. Sliced almonds may be added to the dish if desired.

Nutritional Fact:

Calories: 164.3, Carbohydrates: 21.4 g, Fat: 9.0 g, Protein: 2.3 g, Sodium: 100 mg, Sugars: 26 g

30-Day's Meal Plan

Days	Breakfast	Snacks	Lunch	Dessert	Dinner
1	Green Smoothie	Pumpkin Almond Bites	Leeks Soup	Zesty Zucchini Muffins	Shrimp with White Beans and Feta
2	Artichoke Eggs	Spiced Peanut Butter Apples	Cauliflower Lunch Salad	Grilled Pineapple Strips	Mussels and Chickpea Soup
3	Banana Bread	Roasted Chickpeas	Grilled Veggies with Balsamic	Dates Brownies	Purple Potato Soup
4	Healthy Buckwheat Pancakes	Crab Cake Lettuce Cups	Pasta with Tomatoes and Peas	Strawberry Bruschetta	Vegan Chili
5	Scallions Omelette	Cucumbers Filled with Salmon	Pistachio Mint Pesto Pasta	Frozen Mango Treat	Chunky Tomatoes
6	Apple Oats	Cheese Crackers	Tilapia Casserole	Grapefruit Compote	Quinoa & Bean Fritters
7	Red Velvet Pancakes with Cream Cheese Topping	Zucchini Sticks	Lamb Curry with Tomatoes and Spinach	Pumpkin with Chia Seeds Pudding	Lime Shrimp and Kale
8	Overnight Refrigerated Oatmeal	Oatmeal Cookies	Indian Chicken Stew	Instant Pot Applesauce	Quinoa & Bean Fritters

Days	Breakfast	Snacks	Lunch	Dessert	Dinner
9	Banana Bread	Cucumbers Filled with Salmon	Grilled Veggies with Balsamic	Strawberry Bruschetta	Quinoa & Bean Fritters
10	Scallions Omelette	Roasted Chickpeas	Tilapia Casserole	Pumpkin with Chia Seeds Pudding	Lemon & Herb Grilled Chicken
11	Red Velvet Pancakes with Cream Cheese Topping	Cheese Crackers	Indian Chicken Stew	Instant Pot Applesauce	Chunky Tomatoes
12	Healthy Buckwheat Pancakes	Zucchini Sticks	Mediterranean Potato Salad	Zesty Zucchini Muffins	Vegetarian Lasagna
13	Apple Oats	Pumpkin Almond	Spinach Pork Cubes	Dates Brownies	Mussels and Chickpea Soup
14	Green Smoothie	Spiced Peanut Butter Apples	Leeks Soup	Grapefruit Compote	Shrimp with White Beans and Feta
15	Easy Veggie Muffins	Oatmeal Cookies	Pistachio Mint Pesto Pasta	Grilled Pineapple Strips	Mediterranean Lentil Soup
16	Healthy Buckwheat Pancakes	Crab Cake Lettuce Cups	Stir-Fry Rice with Chicken	Frozen Mango Treat	Stir-Fry Sesame

Days	Breakfast	Snacks	Lunch	Dessert	Dinner
18	Easy Veggie Muffins	Crab Cake Lettuce Cups	Roasted Eggplant Salad	Instant Pot Applesauce	Vegan Chili
19	Eggs on Toast	Roasted Chickpeas	Lamb Curry with Tomatoes and	Grapefruit Compote	Lemon & Herb Grilled Chicken
20	Overnight Refrigerated Oatmeal	Cheese Crackers	Orange Celery Salad	Frozen Mango Treat	Chunky Tomatoes
21	Healthy Buckwheat Pancakes	Zucchini Sticks	Purple Potato Soup	Grilled Pineapple Strips	Vegetarian Lasagna
22	Green Smoothie	Pumpkin Almond	Pistachio Mint Pesto Pasta	Pumpkin with Chia Seeds Pudding	Mussels and Chickpea Soup
23	Apple Oats	Spiced Peanut Butter Apples	Chickpea and Zucchini Salad	Zesty Zucchini Muffins	Shrimp with White Beans and Feta
24	Artichoke Eggs	Roasted Chickpeas	Shrimp with Asparagus	Instant Pot Applesauce	Lime Shrimp and Kale
25	Scallions Omelette	Crab Cake Lettuce Cups	Vegan Tomato and Peanut Stew	Pumpkin with Chia Seeds Pudding	White Bean Soup

Days	Breakfast	Snacks	Lunch	Dessert	Dinner
26	Scallions Omelette	Cheese Crackers	Easy Salmon Steaks	Zesty Zucchini Muffins	Walnuts and Asparagus Delight
27	Red Velvet Pancakes with Cream Cheese Topping	Crab Cake Lettuce Cups	Honey Mustard Salmon	Strawberry Bruschetta	Quinoa & Bean Fritters
28	Overnight Refrigerated Oatmeal	Cucumbers Filled with Salmon	Quinoa and Scallops Salad	Pumpkin with Chia Seeds Pudding	Mussels and Chickpea Soup
29	Healthy Buckwheat Pancakes	Oatmeal Cookies	Cauliflower and Potatoes in Coconut Milk	Instant Pot Applesauce	Lime Shrimp and Kale
30	Eggs on Toast	Pumpkin Almond Bites	Cucumber Chicken Salad with Spicy Peanut Dressing	Grilled Pineapple Strips	Lemon & Herb Grilled Chicken

Dash Diet Cookbook for Beginners

Conclusion

One of the most common ways to lower blood pressure and sugar levels is the Dash diet. The diet is simple to follow and prepare, and it makes use of common grocery store ingredients. However, many people have given up on the Dash diet due to a lack of dish options. Because of this, most people will give up on Dash diet and fall behind until they read this book.

The dash diet should help you feel great, lose weight and have more energy. It's wonderful for ketosis (the process of burning fat for energy) and blood sugar control, and it can keep you regular too! The dash diet is simple and inexpensive. The foods you can eat are delicious, and you don't have to cut out the foods you love. Given the dash diet a try and learn how easy healthy eating can be!

Heart attacks, strokes, heart failure, and some types of cancer can all be reduced with the DASH diet, which has been scientifically demonstrated to be effective. Diabetic complications and kidney stones are both reduced by following the DASH diet plan. The DASH diet emphasizes the need of eating a variety of foods while also ensuring that the key nutrients are being consumed in the correct amounts.

Discovering your love for the Dash diet will be easier by following the process given in this one-of-a-kind cookbook. The recipes are suitable for all levels of cooks, from newbies to experts. All you have to do now is follow the recipes offered in the most easy and self-explanatory manner possible, with the most difficult aspects already taken care of.

The recipes and 30-day meal plans in this book cover a wide range of caloric needs for breakfast, lunch, and dinner. The idea is to help you organize your entire month in advance by recognizing and appreciating how hectic our lives have become today.

The meals are created to help you stay on track with your Dash diet while also providing your body with the nutrients it requires on a daily basis. In addition to helping, you limit your calorie intake, the meals recommended in the book will also be delicious.

If you stick to the diet's basic principles, you'll rapidly see results. Dash diet recipes can be as simple or as complex as you choose; all you need is a cookbook like this one to get started. You'll become an expert in Dash diet cuisine in no time with these recipes! Nutritious food doesn't have to be tasteless or boring to be healthy. This cookbook teaches you how to prepare delicious meals that are also good for you. If you're looking for a wide variety of recipes that you're sure to enjoy, this book is the one for you.

I'd like to thank you and congratulate you for making it all the way through my lines. Thank you for taking the time to read and consider what I have to say. After reading this book, you should have a clearer picture of the DASH diet. After that, you'll need to gather the appropriate ingredients and test out the recipes in this book. To get the most out of the diet, combine it with regular exercise and a healthy lifestyle. I wish you the best of luck in your endeavors!

83

Measurement Conversion Chart

Dry measurement (Volume equivalent):

US STANDARD	METRIC (APPROXIMATE)`
⅛ teaspoon	0.5 mL
¼ teaspoon	1 mL
½ teaspoon	2 mL
¾ teaspoon	4 mL
1 teaspoon	5 mL
1 tablespoon	15 mL
¼ cup	59 mL
⅓ cup	79 mL
½ cup	118 mL
⅔ cup	156 mL
¾ cup	177 mL
1 cup	235 mL
2 cups or 1 pint	475 mL
3 cups	700 mL

4 cups or 1 quart	1 L

Liquid measurement (Volume equivalent):

US STANDARD	US STANDARD (OUNCES)	METRIC (APPROXIMATE)`
2 tablespoons	1 fl. oz.	30 mL
¼ cup	2 fl. oz.	60 mL
⅓ cup	4 fl. oz.	120 mL
1 cup	8 fl. oz.	240 mL
1½ cups	12 fl. oz.	355 mL
2 cups or 1 pint	16 fl. oz.	475 mL
4 cups or 1 quart	32 fl. oz.	1 L
1 gallon	128 fl. oz.	4 L

Weight Equivalents:

US STANDARD	METRIC (APPROXIMATE)`
½ ounce	½ ounce 15 g
1 ounce	1 ounce 30 g
2 ounces	2 ounces 60 g
4 ounces	4 ounces 115 g
8 ounces	8 ounces 225 g
12 ounces	12 ounces 340 g
16 ounces or 1 pound	16 ounces or 1 pound 455 g

Oven Temperature:

FAHRENHEIT (F)	CELSIUS (C) (APPROXIMATE)
250°	120°
300°	150°
325°	165°
350°	180°
375°	190°
400°	200°
425°	220°
450°	230°

Index

W

Walnuts and Asparagus Delight, 30

White Bean Soup, 53

White Sauce, 62

Z

Zesty Zucchini Muffins, 74

Zucchini Sticks, 66

Made in the USA
Coppell, TX
26 February 2023

13433721R00050